Praise for

WHISKEY & YOGA: FIND YOUR PURPOSE

"In David's book **Whiskey & Yoga** I found myself gaining awareness into my own mode of operation! It's rare for me to feel inspired from page one of a book these days, but David hit the nail on the inspired head! If you want a fulfilling and abundant life, then check out this book!"

> ~ Scarlet Ravin, International Best Selling Author of *Follow the Medicine, Awakening Self-Empowerment*

"We all have free will; it's just unfortunate that most of us do not exercise this on a conscious and regular basis. Let David Richards show you how to turn that around in his new book **Whiskey & Yoga**, how to focus on creating the life that you want, and lead you to the freedom that you deserve. An interesting read."

> ~ Joanne Ong, International Best Selling Author of *The Sun Within: Rediscover You*

"**Whiskey & Yoga** is a great guide to finding your purpose. With clear voice and positive import, David Richards illustrates exactly how to transform impossible daydreams into achievable goals. He gets to the heart of this vital topic with insight and clarity. I was really encouraged and inspired and believe you will be too once you read it. I enjoyed it thoroughly and highly recommend it."

> ~ Judy O'Beirn, International Bestselling Author & Creator of the *Unwavering Strength* series

FIND YOUR PURPOSE

WHISKEY & YOGA

Kelsey,
Thanks for your
partnership. Great working
with you.

DAVID RICHARDS

For Ann Elise

Find your Purpose, my beautiful daughter.

TABLE OF CONTENTS

INTRODUCTION   8

PART ONE: WHISKEY

1. GET ME OUTTA THIS CASK!   12
   Whiskey's Origins   17
   Yoga, East to West   18
   Contained Spirits   19

2. THE HAPPINESS BUZZ   20
   Workplace Happy   24
   The Smartphone Tug   27
   Shopping Ourselves Happy   29
   The Drinking Hangover   31
   Productive Happiness   33

3. CONSUMPTION OVERLOAD TO GO, PLEASE   35
   Think About it   37
   The Habit of Distraction   39
   The Lighthouse   40
   The Lighthouse II   42
   Mental Junk Food   44
   Almost Committed   48

4. GIMME A DOUBLE-SHOT OF TRUTH, NEAT!   50
   Truth and Choices   52
   "Try Harder"   55

Digging In   58
Bigger Than Ourselves   60
Your Purpose   61

5. DECISIONS ON THE ROCKS   63
Decisions, Decisions   65
Pushing Through Impossibility   67
Seeking Discomfort   69
The Art of Uncomfort   71
Habits and Emotions   72
Your Purpose Sherpa   75

PART TWO: YOGA

6. OM-M-G, YOU NEED A PLAN   78
The Law   80
Over Reliance on a Plan   82
Define Your Purpose   83

7. DHYANA CHECK OUT MY ASANA?   90
Perception and Reality   93
Spinning Plates   96
Desire and Action   98
Mind Matters   99
Abundance   101

8. I HAVE GANESH ON SPEED-DIAL   102
Seasonal Gratitude   104
Complaining is Maintaining   106
Gratitude as Daily Ritual   107
Gratitude and Purpose   109
The Basic Personality Types   111
Purpose and Disruption   112

9. I HAVE SOMETHING IN MY THIRD EYE!   113
Let it Go   116
Emotions and Intellect   118
Stay on Purpose   119

10. EMBRACE THE POSSIBLE   122

ACKNOWLEDGEMENTS   124

NOTES   125

ABOUT THE AUTHOR   129

INTRODUCTION

Several months ago, I had a memorable conversation with the cashier at my local hardware store. We started the discussion sharing what we both did to stay in shape, but it ended with him confessing that he was still searching for his purpose in life. He was 71 years old. I remember being both sad and happy for him. Sad that he hadn't yet found his purpose, but happy that he was still looking.

At 47, I can say I am, and have been, many things. I'm a writer, and a poet. A heavy metal fan. A yoga instructor. An artist. A health-conscious lover of whiskey and fine wine. A Marine and current executive at a technology conglomerate. A father, brother, son, cousin, uncle, Godfather, colleague and friend. A twice divorced, Harley-riding hopeless romantic with giant feet and an even bigger heart, or so I've been told. And it is through these roles and my many experiences over these two score and seven years that I've come to realize something both sad and profound: too many of us are going through life feeling just like that cashier, stuck and unfulfilled. I know, I've been there myself.

What if I told you that you CAN have a life that is rewarding beyond your wildest dreams? More wealth, more fulfillment. The financial freedom to live the life you've always imagined. The landscape we've woven through-out our life's experiences and the challenges we face in our thinking, need a deep overhaul in order to clean the slate before we can tackle the large task of finding one's life's purpose. With this book, I will help you learn what is holding you back, so you can ignite your passion and have a more fulfilling and meaningful life. No matter what your age or current circumstance, it is my hope to help you get there, through *Whiskey and Yoga*.

For all of their differences, at their core, whiskey and yoga share one very important idea: they both involve the interaction between a spirit and a container. For whiskey, that container is the cask in which it ages. For yoga, the container is the human body. And while it's inevitable that the containers will weaken and wither over time, if fermented and cared for, the timeless spirit within has the ability to change, strengthen and even improve as time goes on; some might say, fulfilling its destiny, or finding its purpose.

Now, find a comfortable seated position, take a deep cleansing breath, pour yourself a tall glass of your favorite elixir, and enjoy your journey through *Whiskey and Yoga*.

David Richards

PART ONE:

WHISKEY

ONE
GET ME OUTTA THIS CASK!

*"A good gulp of hot whiskey at bedtime ~
it's not very scientific, but it helps."*

~ Alexander Fleming

Most of us follow a standard, generationally-handed-down script for our lives. My script was served straight-up with a (military) twist. My brother and I were raised by two loving parents, living at various Marine bases over the course of Dad's career. My folks were married for forty-five years until my father's passing eight years ago. He was a career Marine, serving his country for thirty-one years. My brother, proud to follow in Dad's footsteps, served twenty-six. Despite never wanting to be a Marine growing up, I served fifteen. That was my script.

Transitioning out of uniform and into the civilian world is like leaving the Wild West for the big city. As a gunslinger, you're not sure how the skills you learned in the old setting apply to the new one. My father had served in the infantry in Vietnam before switching jobs in the Marines into the field that was the precursor to information technology. After serving five years doing something I truly enjoyed in being an artillery officer, I adopted that script and did the same thing, switching to IT. My reasoning, somewhat uninformed, was simple – carrying a weapon of any kind meant I might be good for a small handful of jobs. Having even rudimentary IT skills would open up the range of possibilities considerably.

A standard script today goes like this: we are born and raised, nowadays as often as not, in a multi-home family or single-parent home. We go through grade school and then navigate the increasingly challenging years of high school. Upon graduation, after spending over a decade with the same group of kids, we say goodbye to all but a few high school pals, and move on to the next 'act' of our life script. Some of us will start working right away, as our parents did, and others will head off to college. It is in this stage of life that our parents encourage us to explore, take chances, and "get it out of our system." As if to suggest what lies ahead is serious business, somewhat daunting, and not all that fun.

Dr. Seuss once said: "*Adults are just obsolete children and the hell with them.*" I couldn't agree more.

In our twenties, or earlier, we become part of the labor force. College graduates and dropouts alike may move back home (if they ever left) in order to suck from the paternal teat a little longer. Others cut the mom and dad umbilical cord more quickly and venture out on their own as soon as they are able. We all want to fast-track getting our own place at this age. Some are more successful than others.

Many of us switch jobs often. Maybe it's because we want more money, we want to do something else, or we want to live somewhere else. It seems we can't sit still, and we're never satisfied. What is it we're after? We keep looking, searching.

Those who are lucky enough will meet someone and fall in love. High school and college sweethearts are as common as romances found online these days. Many scripts involve getting married, buying a house, and having children. Not in any particular order. Many will again switch jobs and buy a larger home.

Some of us will divorce. In fact, many of us have that subplot written into our scripts, statistically speaking. The reasons vary, but they all boil down to one thing; we believe that person or that relationship didn't meet our expectations. For those who take this path with children in the mix, the reality of trying to provide stability for the kids can prove both elusive and difficult. Two households. Two sets of rules. Two hurt and damaged adults trying to navigate these murky waters and figure out where their script leads next, all while trying to detangle it from the script of the ex. It's complicated and messy. We forge ahead.

All of us, whether married, divorced, single, remarried... we all age, and most find a way to "settle in" to our own version of life. All the while, children grow and follow their version of the script, repeating the pattern: grade school, high school, college, marriage, family. When they have children of their own, we find ourselves in the magical world of grand-parenting. I'm not yet a grandparent, but it seems pretty wonderful. I know my daughter has always enjoyed her time with her Nonny and Poppy. And Nonny relishes the role of doting grandmother whenever my daughter comes to visit.

Throughout this process the thinking is, we only get better with age, like a good whiskey. And there's truth in that, for some. Some people "come into their own" and are able to find a truly rich and rewarding life. This may happen easily and early on, or it may happen after they've gone through several life experiences, culminating in a "mid-life crisis," "spiritual awakening," or "finding oneself." For them, there is a moment of transcendence, where a fire seems to ignite, life shifts and dreams manifest into reality. To those looking in, it seems quite seamless, but the truth is, for most, finding one's purpose is a process, and not usually a given.

It is unfortunate that for too many of those people, that fire never ignites. We see glimpses of it in our lives, but bills pile up, kids come along, life gets complicated, and the excuses mount. Instead of living a life of Purpose, we're living life by accident. In these lives, "getting better with age" translates to accepting that this is as good as things are going to get. Acceptance is to surrender. Letting go of the dreams we had. We may shy away from nobler and higher aspirations because that feels scary and, as life advances, we learn through experience to be risk averse. These lives stay "in the cask" in other words. While some may be deluded into thinking that they're still getting better with age, in reality, they're just getting older. They may seek comfort, affirmation and familiarity within their tribes, groups, and friends as they age, settle, and muddle through together. After all, we all want to survive life, right?

I promise you, there is more. You don't have to settle, and you don't have to muddle. If you truly want to, you CAN have a Purpose-filled life that is rewarding beyond your wildest dreams. You can ignite the passion to have a more fulfilling and meaningful life. You can realize your Purpose. The reality is, we all want to lead lives that are more fulfilling. We want a sustained level of happiness. Connecting with our life's Purpose can provide the fulfillment we so desperately seek.

You may be reading this saying, "*Oh, please, that ship has sailed. I'm too old. I'm too settled. I've got a nice thing going. Life is fine, why rock the boat?*" Others may be saying, "*I'm too busy. Are you kidding? Kids have places to go. I've got laundry to fold. There isn't enough time in the day as it is!*" If you're younger, you're thinking, "*I have plenty of time. I can get all deep and introspective and figure that stuff out later.*" It's easy to be complacent. Society wants you to be complacent. Our culture is ready to plug you in to whatever takes your mind off of realizing a more-fulfilled life. And we are all too willing to put self-fulfillment on the back burner. After all, "getting out of the cask" sounds complicated, and a tad uncomfortable, right?

What if I told you that finding your Purpose simply comes down to making different choices? Let me give you an example.

If I say to you, take the next thirty minutes and watch your favorite reality show, or use that thirty minutes to visualize the kind of life you want for yourself. Which choice would you make? On one hand, you get to kick back, relax, and take your mind off of your own reality, by watching someone else's "reality."

This is a pretty safe route. It's mindless entertainment that only requires a modest amount of your attention. That's it. The show's going to happen, whether you watch it or not. It's already been created.

On the other hand, you can start the process of discovering your Purpose, as you visualize the greatness that is possible within your own life. You are in possession of what it is you desire. More wealth than you previously thought possible. The magnificent house or fantastic sports car you've always wanted. Vacationing when and where you want. And in seeing it, feeling it, and visualizing it, you can begin to bring it into your life. Thirty minutes. Your choice.

This option is different. You have to be engaged here. You have to be present. Invested. This hasn't been created. Not yet.

What do you want? Do you even know? Take the time to ask yourself. Do you want financial freedom? A different career? To feel and look healthier? All of the above? What does it take to achieve those dreams?

Without question, we need to spend time thinking about them. If I want to be a millionaire, I need to think like a millionaire. How does a millionaire think? What do they think about? How do they organize their time? I need to think and behave that way too.

Or let's say I want to direct a movie, or become a veterinarian. I need specialized knowledge about how to do these things. I need to get experience and training in that industry. I need to make contacts with folks established in that career. I need to watch what they do, and understand how they think. I need to research and ask questions about how to proceed successfully down that path.

Many of us listen to the self-talk that tries to hold us back. "*I can't do it. I'm too young. I'm too old. I'll probably fail. I don't know how.*" Of course, you don't know how. If you did, you'd be doing it already! Think if your parents had adopted that mentality when it came to getting you potty-trained. "*Sarah hasn't learned to go the bathroom. I guess she'll never figure it out. Time to stock up on the Huggies.*" It's ludicrous. Who wants to buy that many diapers?

Everything in life takes practice. With practice, through repetition, we develop habits. Good ones and bad ones. Habits are nothing more than a product of our thoughts and our decisions. Eventually we become our habits. Habits lead to patterns. There may be misfires along the way. There are sure to be stumbles. But if you put down the remote, or whatever is distracting you from your truth, invest the time and ask the right questions, your Purpose will reveal itself to you. And that's when the magic happens.

"*Alright,*" you're saying. "*Let's say I agree with what you, and I see that you're on to something. I'm trying, I'm reading your book, I'm taking the first step. But what on earth do whiskey and yoga have to do with one another?*" This is an excellent question. At first glance, could there be two more diametrically opposed concepts than whiskey and yoga? I enjoy a nice scotch, but I've never had one before, during, or after I've taught or attended a yoga class. They're rarely on my mind at the same time.

WHISKY'S ORIGINS

The term "whisky" is Gaelic in origin. The original term, *uisge beatha*, means water of life. The art of distillation is believed to have arrived in Scotland and Ireland by the 15th Century. Initially, the distillation process was medicinal in nature, with the first mention of whisky production in Scotland surfacing in the 1494 edition of the *Exchequer Rolls*, the government's accounting office.

Sometime before 1541, King Henry VIII of England dissolved the monasteries, which up until that point had a monopoly on whisky production. This moved production into individual homes. Distillation was still in its early stages; whisky was not allowed to age. The taste of it was raw and unrefined.

The wooden cask in which whiskey is aged is crucial for providing flavor and spiciness. Three main compounds – lignin, vanillin, and lactones – providing a whiskey with its vanilla, buttery, and coconut flavors. American oaks have a higher concentration of lactones than do European oaks, and therefore have a stronger coconut-like flavor. Spice is derived from tannins which, if whiskey is aged too long, can overtake the flavor compounds and make the whiskey taste less than desirable. Finally, it's worth noting that "whisky" refers to Scotch, or those fine spirits that originate from Scotland. "Whiskey" refers to the rest of the world.

Would you believe there are health benefits to drinking whiskey? It's true. Whiskey is full of ellagic acid, a powerful antioxidant which breaks up free radicals in the body and helps reduce the risk of cancer. Additionally, studies have shown that the ellagic acid found in whiskey plays a factor in delaying the onset of dementia. These benefits are yielded from drinking whiskey in moderation. Additional benefits include managing the body's insulin and glucose levels, minimizing the likelihood of diabetes. Further studies show benefits in heart health, weight management, and in boosting the immune system.

YOGA, EAST TO WEST

In contrast, Yoga is a collection of spiritual, mental, and physical disciplines hailing out of ancient India. Its origins date back to between the sixth and fifth centuries BCE, but it was only introduced to the West around the turn of the 20th century. In the 1980's, yoga gained popularity across the Western world as a program of physical exercise. In gyms across the U.S. that remains true. Over the past few decades, yoga studios that cater to the meditative and spiritual aspects of yoga have sprung up coast to coast.

There are more than a dozen styles of yoga regularly practiced today, from well-known styles such as hatha, kundalini, and ashtanga, to more niche styles like nude yoga, senior yoga, and acro yoga.

The benefits of yoga are many. They range from increased flexibility and muscle strength, to better athletic performance and weight loss. A regular yoga practice also reduces the chance of injury and is good for cardio and circulatory health.

CONTAINED SPIRITS

Both yoga and whiskey are spiritual journeys, of sorts. Both pursue a kind of enlightenment. For whiskey, there is a point where the flavor has reached its peak, and staying in the cask longer will not yield a sharper taste. For yoga, the enlightenment is a path towards understanding the inner-connectedness of everything and everyone. When pursued in moderation, both can have the same pleasing effects on the body: reflection, relaxation, and bliss. There are almost as many flavor combinations of whiskey as there are styles of yoga to practice. Whiskeys can be smoky or delicate, rich or light. Yoga can be flow-y or slow, rote or varied. And while I don't recommend practicing both at the same time, "Beer Yoga" has already become an international trend, so maybe we're on the verge of a new movement! I'll have to make sure that when people search for "Whiskey Yoga" on the internet, this book lands in the top five results. I understand there's a bar in Austin, Texas where you can have a shot while directly behind you, people are working their downward dog.

Back to Purpose. Before we get to igniting your flame, it's critical to understand the landscape we face in getting there. I'm not going to lie; challenges and big changes lie ahead. Becoming aware of the script you have been following, redirecting your inner voice, changing your habits, and staying focused are essential tools in cleaning the slate and preparing for your Purpose. Are you ready?

TWO:

THE HAPPINESS BUZZ

"The purpose of life is not to be happy.
It is to be useful, to be honorable, to be compassionate, to have
made some difference that you lived and lived well."

~ Alexander Fleming

Childhood is a magical time. This past Easter, I attended an Easter egg hunt with my Goddaughter's family. She's still in preschool and didn't have a care in the world that day. As I was pushing her on her swing, she was telling me about the picture she'd taken with a unicorn earlier that morning. She said there were two other unicorns, but they'd gone missing, and that she didn't know where they were. She then jumped off the swing and informed me we were going to have to go up into the playhouse to find the unicorns. I happily obliged. She told me it was "okay" after I bumped my head on the small entryway into her playhouse. Despite out best efforts, we didn't find the missing unicorns, but we certainly had a fun time searching. She was a happy camper.

In childhood, the imagination is free to run wild, like a prancing unicorn through fields of daisies. It is unfettered by the constraints that are imposed when conventional schooling starts. It is happiness unbound. No wonder kids are so eager to be home from school. In Western culture, we shut down their imagination and channel their focus towards learning how to be "successful" based on an education system's definition of success.

More than that, we educate them that failure is something to be avoided. No one gets congratulated coming in the door with a report card of straight "F's".

In childhood, happiness seems so accessible. It's right there. Everyone has either personally experienced, or heard the story about the child who opens their presents at Christmas and is happier playing with the box in which the present was packed, rather than the present itself. A cardboard box makes us happy!

As we get older, something changes. We say goodbye to our imagination, and we do our best to embrace the reality of everyday life. We find happiness in snippets. Happiness becomes a pursuit, something we have to chase. Why is happiness evading us? Does it not like us anymore? Was it something we said?

Our pursuit of happiness is met with success occasionally, but the happiness is short-lived. We get a job we like and find happiness. After a while, the happiness fades. We get a promotion, and that registers on the happiness scale for a time. We go on vacation, and that makes us happy. But the vacation ends, and we have to go back to having our nose on the grindstone.

We get happy buying things. Sometimes we feel bad about buying them, and we short-circuit the happiness we were after. We meet someone and fall in love. That makes us happy. And then it doesn't.

In re-reading the Emerson quote at the beginning of this chapter, something feels off. We shouldn't be happy? That seems counter-intuitive. Are happiness and usefulness mutually exclusive? If we shouldn't be happy, why do we spend so much time and energy pursuing happiness? Why do we enjoy being happy, and seeing others happy around us?

Emerson also said, *"Happiness is a perfume you cannot pour on others without getting some on yourself."* He clearly saw something worthwhile in happiness. But what is happiness?

If we look to the Greeks and ancient philosophy, we find that happiness is not simply an emotion, but a notion. It's the good life, it's a kind of prosperity. This leads us to ask, should we be happy all the time? Don't we need a little rain in our lives to appreciate the sun? We do.

If we need to feel other emotions to appreciate happiness, then happiness is not a destination. It really is meant to be part of the journey.

There are two elements to happiness. The first is the level of satisfaction we find with our lives, while the second is how we actually feel on a day-to-day basis. If we take all of this and bundle it together, happiness is feeling satisfied with the quality of our living and feeling happy more often than not. With that understanding, how does the body interpret and create happiness?

Science tells us there are four hormones in the body that make up what we know as happiness: endorphins, serotonin, oxytocin, and dopamine.

Need your endorphin fix? Get to the gym, lift weights! These are the body's natural painkillers. Originally, endorphins helped our ancestors outrun the things that wanted to make a meal out of them. We can increase our endorphins with an anaerobic workout or, for the more adventurous, by eating spicy foods. When we eat spicy foods, the tongue tells the brain this feels like pain, and the brain responds with endorphins.

If weightlifting isn't your thing, but you're still looking for a happiness boost from your workout, a low-intensity workout (yoga anyone?) will release serotonin into the body. Serotonin is the "happiest" of hormones, in that it makes us sociable, manages our moods, and keeps depression at bay. When we soak in the sun's rays, the resulting Vitamin D produced in the body triggers the release of serotonin. Thinking happy thoughts also releases serotonin, as does consuming foods containing tryptophan. The body converts tryptophan to serotonin.

Oxytocin, otherwise known as the love hormone, is released during sex and childbirth. It is also released with other types of affectionate physical contact, like hugging. This realization explains why "cuddle parties" have become a thing. A massage feels so good because it also releases oxytocin. If you want to increase your daily oxytocin, become more affectionate with friends and family. Oxytocin also helps us establish trust.

Dopamine is the pleasure hormone. It keeps us alert and mentally sharp. When we accomplish a goal, the sense of satisfaction we get comes from dopamine. What kind of goals release dopamine?

Household chores… checking off the items on that to-do list on the kitchen counter. Mowing the grass, folding the laundry, or cleaning out the garage. For the working-class, incremental goals are found in an abundance at work. It's the long-term program we're responsible for, or the near-term project we're on. We complete these tasks and assignments, and feel a sense of satisfaction and happiness.

As with most things in life, too much of a good thing has its downside. If our bodies constantly released endorphins, we would push ourselves too hard and risk serious injury. With a constant supply of oxytocin, we'd trust everyone indiscriminately and end up being the person who buys the Brooklyn Bridge. Too much dopamine leads to addiction, and would short-circuit our ability to meaningfully prioritize goals.

Happiness is different than fulfillment. Where happiness is focused on the good life and feeling well, happy, fulfillment is about achieving something. That's why we feel good when we give of our time to a worthy cause, something greater than ourselves. The greater the task and sense of effort required to achieve something, the greater the sense of fulfillment once it's achieved. What greater fulfillment than fulfilling our life's Purpose?

For a great many of us, these two emotions most intertwine in our place of business.

WORKPLACE HAPPY

Johann Wolfgang von Goethe said, *"The human race is a monotonous affair. Most people spend the greatest part of their time working in order to live, and what little freedom remains so fills them with fear that they seek out any and every means to be rid of it."*

According to the U.S. Bureau of Labor Statistics Spotlight on Statistics report from 2015, 15 million Americans were self-employed, representing 10.1 percent of all U.S. Employment. That means for the other 133 million working Americans, we're working for someone else.

Working for someone else has its benefits. Salaries can be decent, most companies offer solid health benefits, even ergonomic workspaces. Socializing has evolved beyond the traditional office party and company picnics. Offices today can have free soft drinks and coffee or tea, pool tables, ping pong tables, and even video games.

Besides sleep, most of our time is spent working for someone else, in companies both large and small.

Cliff Oxford, the founder of the Oxford Center For Entrepreneurs, boils workplace happiness down to two kinds: H.R. Happy and High Performance Happy. He defines H.R. Happy bosses as those who are "at least superficially nice and periodically pretend to be interested in employees as people." In other words, H.R. Happy is geared towards enabling Human Resource to attract the best talent, but the happiness is superficial or cursory at best.

Oxford goes on to say that High Performance Happy is an "attitude with a skill set that says we are on a mission that is bigger than any one of us." While H.R. Happy is focused on doing what pleases us, High Performance Happy is scrappy, focusing on fighting tooth and nail. It is centered around what you are giving, not what you are taking.

In my coaching practice, I like to say there are two kinds of coaching: there's coaching someone to love what they do, and then there's coaching someone to do what they love. In my experience, these are very different ideas, and for most of us, Corporate America spends millions of dollars on the former.

Businesses have a vested interest in seeing their employees happy. Happy employees, the thinking goes, are more cooperative and more productive. That helps the bottom-line. But why do we work in the first place?

We work because everyone else is doing it. Our education system is based on preparing us for work. If we pay large sums of money to universities or are fortunate enough to get a scholarship, we get some official seal of approval that suggests we're ready for work, perhaps even entitled to more pay for our work.

We work because it's a form of socializing. We come together in teams to get things done. Even when we're working independently, there are numerous chances throughout the day to connect with someone.

We work for the sense of responsibility. If we're in charge, this is empowering. It can also be stressful. But when we accomplish something, we become fulfilled.

When we join the workforce, it's a question of finding out what we like to do. Simply matching our skills to the "right" job. Once again, companies will spend exorbitant sums of money to run evaluations such as Meyers-Briggs, StrengthFinders, and any number of other tests in order that you, the employee, might understand your work-self better, and that managers might position you in roles that you'll find most rewarding.

But something doesn't make sense. When we look at some people who have been wildly successful in life, we find something interesting. What do Steve Jobs, Kevin Rose, Richard Branson, and Rachael Ray all have in common? They don't have a university diploma hanging on their wall.

Did Steve Jobs love what he did? It seems he did, yes. But it clearly seems he was doing what he loved. If he were alive today, I wonder if he would consider what he was doing at Apple "work"? Does Richard Branson work? Or Rachael Ray? I know they're incredibly productive people who've impacted perhaps millions of lives, but their "work" feels very different from the work most of us are familiar with. What is their "job"?

We work to survive. These days, our basic needs are met easily. We have bills to pay. Obligations to be met. We work to make our lives better. For many of us, we work to retire. Isn't that a strange concept? We work, so that we can stop working and live life. The thinking goes, if we work harder, our efforts may translate to a pay raise, or promotion, which means we can retire sooner.

At Cisco over the last year, there's been an increased focus on teams, and what makes up strong teams. We've done meaningful work with The Marcus Buckingham Group. During the course of this training, some alarming information has been shed on the American workforce.

Do you like the show *The Walking Dead*? I'm guessing you do, because according to today's *Gallup Daily* report on U.S. Employee Engagement, 68% of us are zombies, mindlessly going through our days, with no real energy devoted to our work. Said differently, only 32% of employees in the U.S. are enthusiastic about their work and their workplace. In the rest of the world, that number is 13%. Almost 90% of the working world is doing something they'd rather not be doing. In an effort to counter this, many companies try to connect with their local communities.

We feel happy when we give back to the community. If we're involved in building homes with Habitat for Humanity, or volunteering at the local food bank or SPCA, the dopamine is flowing when we accomplish these well-meaning tasks. We feel good about ourselves, and we feel good about our company for having the compassion to support such endeavors.

There's another dopamine generator that most of us have nearby all the time. Pick up your smartphone.

THE SMARTPHONE TUG

Ever get caught up playing a game on your phone? Feels good to finally get past that level you've been struggling with for the past few days, doesn't it? The game is built to reward you, and to keep you playing. Why am I talking about online gaming? Aren't games for kids? In 2016, the average age of an online gamer was 35 years of age. I've got games on my phone. I'm betting you do too.

What about when you post a photo online and your friends and family "like" it? That's triggering the release of dopamine in your body. Is it really any surprise then when you get in line at your nearest coffee shop, the bank, or *anywhere a line forms*, you see people's heads craned looking down at their smartphones? It's a happiness-machine.

I remember several years ago when I saw one of the first online games appear on Facebook. The game was a vampire game, and as a player, you had to complete tasks in order to level up your vampire. There were perks or boosts you could give your vampire to make him stronger, which would potentially give you a leg up on your rival vampires. You just had to pay money for these perks, as little as ninety-nine cents, or as much as ninety-nine dollars. I remember what an odd concept the idea seemed at the time. People were going to pay real money for an imaginary perk online in a world that didn't exist? Would this really catch on? It caught on. In a massive way.

In their Global Games Market Report released in April 2017, *Newzoo* shows that 2.2 billion gamers across the world are forecast to generate $108.9 billion in game revenues in 2017, representing an increase of $7.8 billion dollars from 2016. Digital games, or games that are played on a mobile device, computer, or video game console represent 87% or $94.4 billion of the global market. Within that number, Mobile is the most lucrative segment. Since 2016, smartphone and tablet gaming has grown an impressive 19% year over year to $46.1 billion, or 42% of the overall gaming market.

Think about that for a minute in comparison to going to the movies. Hollywood pours months of time, sometimes years, and incredible man-hours, money, and technology to produce some of your favorite movies. I'm a huge superhero movie fan. I grew up reading comics and am happy to give my money to the movie theaters to see *Thor* and *Hulk* slug it out. Or to see *Warner Brothers* try to figure out how to successfully bring *Batman, Superman*, and the rest of the DC universe to the big screen. These movies are typically juggernauts at the box office, and linchpins that serve as make-or-break bellwethers for the large studios during the calendar year.

Since 2008, when stunned audiences embraced Robert Downey Jr's portrayal of *Iron Man*, Marvel Entertainment has made just under $11 billion dollars. In the past year, online gaming grew at a rate that nearly equaled Marvel Entertainment's purse from the last ten years of movie-making.

Technology isn't responsible for all our woes, but ask yourself... are you controlling your tech, or is your tech controlling you? Is *Angry Birds* making you angry?

SHOPPING OURSELVES HAPPY

Is the release of dopamine from technology limited to gaming? Think about how easy it is to buy online. With one or two clicks of a button, you can buy something on eBay or Amazon, or any number of online retailers. Sounds like the makings of an incremental goal. And what's the key phrase with dopamine? *One more.*

According to the annual survey published in June of 2016 by analytics firm comScore and UPS, shoppers are doing more than half of their shopping online, a figure that has steadily increased year after year. And why not? As of January 2017, Amazon sells 398,040,250 million products. If you know what you want, you can order it *within seconds.*

Why do we buy the things we buy? Sometimes it's for status. If I buy a certain type of sports car, or certain brand of clothes, then the thinking goes, people associate me with those brands. The status defined by a product is a function of how the product is marketed. On average, companies spend 10% of their revenue on marketing, though for some software companies, the marketing budget is over half their revenue!

Buying things changes our mood. If we make buying something a goal, when we accomplish that goal, our friend dopamine greets us with a sense of accomplishment, a sense of well-being. A sense of happiness.

Buying things makes us feel good. When compared with the conventional manner in which we used to buy things… going to a store… buying something online has started to feel like an incremental goal. There's no walking down aisles to see if what you're after is in stock. No checkout lines. You find what you're looking for, put it in your "cart" and presto! If it's an online store you've shopped at before, odds are that you're a member and have a saved profile, which includes your shipping and billing information, and your credit card. What once entailed a car trip, packing up the family or picking up friends along the way, finding a parking spot, and then physically going into the store can now be done from our laptop, our tablet. Even our phones.

THE DRINKING HANGOVER

For some of us, our pursuit of situational happiness has stayed the same since college, or high school. It became an enjoyable part of the script at an early age, so why change? Thursday night at the bars? No harm, no foul. Friday night binge-drinking with the guys? What's the big deal? We enjoyed those things when we were young, and they stuck. Sure, it takes a little more time to recover now than when we were in our 20's (if you're reading this and in your 20's, congrats!), but it's still fun. We're "happy" at the time we do it, even if we pay for it the next day. Or the rest of the weekend if we're old enough.

We vow not to do that again. And that thinking holds true... until the next weekend.

We want to enjoy ourselves, especially when we work at a job we don't really feel all that enthused about, which is nearly 70% of us in the U.S. We deserve a good time! If we think through that idea, we're now indulging in something to spite the job that provides us the money to indulge in the first place.

You may be saying, *"David, the name of your book is Whiskey and Yoga... WHISKEY... are you really going there?"* I enjoy a glass of whiskey after work some evenings. Guilty. But binge drinking is another matter.

Binge drinking is defined as the consumption of an excessive amount of alcohol in a short period of time. According to a recent Harvard School of Public Health College Alcohol Study, two out of five college students are binge drinkers. 51% of male students drink five or more drinks in a row, while 40% of female students drink four or more drinks consecutively.

We drink to escape ourselves. Sometimes it works, and we are less in our heads about what's wrong with us, or what we don't like about ourselves. In those moments, we feel great. How many of us have told a friend, *"I love you man!"* after having a few too many drinks?

In some cases, we don't make the escape. Alcohol weighs us down, and we get caught up in our thoughts or insecurities, leaving us moody and even hostile.

Generally speaking, alcohol elevates our moods because it reduces cognitive thought. We drink to unwind, to let our hair down. Outrageous behavior can be dismissed because of alcohol. It calls to mind Frank the Tank from the movie *Old School* who, after reluctantly chugging beers with college students, decides it's a good idea to go streaking down to the quad. Even when his wife pulls up alongside him in her car, he is undeterred. Though he is alone in running naked down the street, he matter-of-factly tells his wife, "*Honey, we're streaking.*" If outrageous behavior can't be dismissed, at least it can be accounted for.

Ironically, there's something else that alcohol has in common with yoga beyond the spirit-in-a-container idea. Both can provide a transcendent experience. When we feel the euphoric buzz of alcohol that precedes getting wasted, we feel unity with our friends, we feel the goodness that is living. We feel connected, and one. I know if you're a practitioner of yoga, you're jumping out of your asana right about now... I'm not saying alcohol is an expression of prana! I am saying that alcohol, like yoga, can allow us to be present.

But alcohol, like the fixes we get from accomplishing our incremental goals, provides us a hollow kind of happiness. The sad truth is, alcohol and technology seem to converge at addiction, even though we don't yet fully grasp how addicting technology can be.

PRODUCTIVE HAPPINESS

I think back to my time in Somalia in support of OPERATION RESTORE HOPE. I was part of the initial landing force. We'd been told to expect resistance at the beach. Up to one thousand armed Somalis might be waiting for us. Fear was a co-pilot, whispering incessantly in my ear about everything that could go wrong as we approached the pitch-black shore. Was the initial landing scary? Yes, right up until the television camera lights came on.

The MEU stayed in Somalia for two months. During that time, we provided security for food convoys, supported Navy dentists and doctors in treating Somalis for illness and dental care. I remember carrying a two-year old little boy across a bridge during one of the medical/dental missions. I offered him a bottle of water and he hugged me. Over a bottle of clean water.

By the beginning of February 1993, enough Army and Marine Corps units had arrived from the states that the MEU was no longer needed ashore. But was that time fulfilling? Absolutely. Was I happy? I missed being away from home for the holidays, but I was very happy. It was what I've come to call "Productive Happiness," or the PH Scale. This scale can be used to assess the relative value of productivity of something that we do to make us happy.

Giving back to others? That's a 10 on the PH Scale. Playing a game on your smartphone or tablet? A 2, and only because the game may provide some hand-eye coordination benefits. A movie could be range anywhere from a 2-8. If it's a mindless movie, or even (gasp!) a superhero movie, it might be somewhere between a 2 and a 4. If it's a documentary, the score could be upwards of 8. The PH Scale is subjective, but operates on the idea that there is a universally accepted view on the general productivity value of the things we do every day.

Perhaps Emerson is on to something. If we define happiness through some lens of self-indulgence, that is no great purpose.

We deserve happiness. There's no question in my mind on the matter. The challenge is, we seem to fill our days with low-grade happiness that leaves us unsatisfied and constantly searching for more. Our consumption habits in today's world don't do much to help us.

THREE:
CONSUMPTION OVERLOAD
TO GO, PLEASE

Your time is limited, so don't waste it living someone else's life.
Don't be trapped by dogma – which is
living with the results of other people's thinking.

Don't let the noise of others' opinions drown out your own
inner voice. And most important, have the courage to
follow your heart and intuition.

~ Steve Jobs

While in the Marine Corps, I was fortunate enough to be selected to attend a special school called the School of Advanced Warfighting, or SAW. SAW was the second-year program after Command and Staff College (CSC), which prepares field grade officers, Majors in this case, to be assigned to regimental and division staffs.

SAW went a step further. Though up to two hundred officers applied, only twenty-four were selected. Most of the twenty-four were Marines, but we had some army and air force officers, as well as a handful of international officers. I hadn't even heard of SAW until I spoke with my CSC faculty leader. He suggested I apply, so I did, and was ecstatic when I got accepted. He later relayed to me that, as part of my application package, he had submitted some of my poetry.

Regarding SAW, the Marine Corps University website states "the school educates officers in capabilities, limitations and requirements of military institutions and the application of that knowledge to improve war-fighting capabilities of nations. The curriculum is taught by progressive studies considering the framework for military institutions and how nations prepare for war." Heady stuff.

The school was beyond belief. In addition to the brilliant faculty, we had guest speakers that included accomplished historians, the media, and a Supreme Court justice. During the course of the school year, we journeyed to Europe and Vietnam to study historic battlefields as a means of better understanding why the commanders at those battles had made the decisions they'd made.

The first week of school really set the tone. We were given a speed-reading course, and tested daily to assess how much how reading was improving. We needed it too, because our reading assignments were daunting. I was "head" of the class with a 1200 words per minute speed.

We met either Monday and Wednesday, or Tuesday and Thursday for class time, typically from 0730 – 1200. On the days we didn't meet, our reading assignments ranged from a few hundred pages to entire books. More importantly, there was "chin-scratching" time built in. This was time to allow us to think and reflect on what we'd read, as well as what had been discussed during the live classroom sessions.

That chin-scratching time was one of the greatest gifts I've received in my professional career, and seemingly a novel concept when you look at how much we consume information-wise today.

Were you working when the internet-age dawned? I was stationed at Camp Pendleton, California when the first big, boxy computer arrived for our unit. Every day we would print out the daily report on how many Marines were present that day. Then, someone would walk it across the large parade deck that separated our unit from our headquarters unit.

Within a few years, every desk had its own workstation. Internet and email was going to revolutionize work. All the meetings we had, all the phone calls we had to make... all could be summed up in an email and conversations would be transformed. We seemed destined to give ourselves back hours in the day. But what happened?

WHISKEY AND YOGA: *Find Your Purpose*

THINK ABOUT IT

The Argentine philosopher and physicist Mario Bunge once said, "*We all would like to know more and, at the same time, to receive less information. In fact, the problem of a worker in today's knowledge industry is not the scarcity of information but its excess. The same holds for professionals: just think of a physician or an executive, constantly bombarded by information that is at best irrelevant. In order to learn anything, we need time. And to make time we must use information filters allowing us to ignore most of the information aimed at us. We must ignore much to learn a little.*"

The constant barrage of information today reminds me of my first trip to New York City, back in 2005. I was staying in New Jersey, and arrived at my hotel just as dusk was settling in. After a ferry ride and short subway excursion, I found myself coming up from the subway station right in the middle of Times Square. The lights, the cars, the people. It was all too much. My senses were overwhelmed. I headed into a nearby restaurant to collect myself before venturing back out.

That feels like the world we live in today. We are constantly bombarded with information. We get in our cars with the radio talking, or music playing. We get to work and are inundated with emails, meetings, and conferences. Surfing the web for information, we struggle to navigate through the click-bait and pop-up ads. Coming home, after dinner we tune in to catch up on our latest TV shows, all the while checking and answering emails, responding to texts, or checking some other form of social media.

It's starting to feel like Neo and the *Matrix*. The key difference is, where Neo's actual body was in a liquid-filled cocoon, and he was "living" in a computer program (sorry if I just ruined the movie... it's a modern classic. You should have seen it by now.) Our cocoon is in our back pocket, our purse, or on the table. And that's only when it's not in front of our faces, or workstations at our desk.

Studies today show that the average teenager spends nine hours a day on their smartphone. If we're generous and say they're being attentive during school, this suggests they're spending more time on their phone than they are doing anything else. In other words, we're programming our children to be drones.

Are we much better as adults? We seem to feel like if we don't have our phone with us in line, we aren't being productive. As you walk in to your local coffee shop or fast food restaurant, stop and notice how many people in line are looking down at their phones.

As adults, we do things that actually make us unhappy. We have another piece of cake, even though we know we shouldn't. The next day, we look at ourselves angrily in the mirror. We have one more drink for the road, symbolically thumbing our nose at the idea of drinking and driving. We buy things we don't need. Why do we do these things? Part of it is "habit and ritual… staying true to our script. It's the pattern. Part of it is, we don't think.

Johann Wolfgang von Goethe said, *"Thinking is easy, acting is difficult, and to put one's thoughts into action is the most difficult thing in the world."* Today, we live in such a reactionary world, it seems as though thinking hasn't gotten harder, just more elusive.

We've gotten to a weird place where we presume that the basic cognitive processes of everyday life – remembering someone's phone number, day-dreaming about an upcoming vacation, or perceiving our surroundings equates to actual thinking. Keeping appointments, staying on top of meetings, getting the kids to soccer practice… these things represent navigating a schedule, not thinking.

Is remembering someone's phone number the same thing as problem solving, or reflecting on a thoughtful passage we read in a book? I would contend it isn't. Perceiving our surroundings isn't something we actively do; our mind does it for us. I don't need to actively say in my head, *"The trees are green"* to know the trees are green. I see it, and instinctively know it.

We're going through our days on "autopilot" only to wake up in the middle of our lives thinking, *"how the hell did I get here?"*

THE HABIT OF DISTRACTION

Our habits become our lives.

Sorry. My cellphone buzzed. What was I saying?

THE LIGHTHOUSE

Words matter. Today, we have taken a casual approach to maintaining the integrity of words and their meaning. What am I talking about? *Today was the best day ever! Billy is probably the funniest person on the face of the planet. That is the most ridiculous thing I've ever heard.*

We're all given to a level of hyperbole in our use of language, but this hyperbole underscores something deeper. We're cannibalizing the true meaning of words, and in doing so, impairing real understanding. Losing understanding is like having two pieces of rope that we intend to tie together, but never do. And yet, inexplicably, we leave the ropes thinking they're tied together. It doesn't make sense. We have literally changed the meaning of the word "literally". Where it once used to mean "in a literal sense" it now is used as a point of emphasis. *He is literally the dumbest person I've ever met... did you see LeBron in that game last night? He was literally on fire. A Triple Double!* Here's another example.

I was talking with someone the other day. At one point during the conversation, this person made the comment, *"but my mind was wandering".* I thought to myself, that isn't true. Your mind wasn't wandering. Your awareness was wandering.

The mind is this vast ocean of thoughts, memories, and recollections. Awareness is a lighthouse. It shines focus on different parts of the mind. Think of your high school graduation. Or the last concert you went to. Think of the last person you spoke with. Your lighthouse has been guided to those memories in the ocean of your mind.

The lighthouse is awareness. Awareness is presence. During yoga classes, I ask students to be present. That's why we focus on the breath. No one thinks about the breath they took five minutes ago, or the breath they're going to take in an hour. Focusing on breathing helps us stay present. The aspiration is to be present, without thinking. In other words, just to be.

When we want to understand how to overcome distraction or how to concentrate better, we need to understand the relationship between the ocean and the lighthouse. If we think our mind is always wandering, we don't understand how the mind works. If the mind is indeed wandering like some dog on the streets, how can we control it? We can't. We just have to hope at some point it comes back to us. The point is, if we don't understand how the mind works, our efforts to address distraction and concentration will be challenged. We'll leave the ropes untied while proclaiming success.

THE LIGHTHOUSE II

In my coaching practice, I've come to appreciate some words that are better than others when it comes to asking a client a question. Ideally, I want to ask an open-ended question that helps the client move forward in what they're looking for out of our session.

"How" is strong. "What" is another great starter. Like, "*what does success look like?*" or "*what if you looked at it differently?*" Conversely, "have" is low on my list of words to lead with. "*Have you thought of this?*" puts me in the position of proposing a solution to the client, and that's not what coaching is about. "Why" is borderline. If used in the wrong context, it can put a client on the defensive.

This led me to thinking about the questions we ask ourselves. We beat ourselves up, especially when we make mistakes. "*Why did I do that? I'm so stupid!*" or "*Why does this always happen to me?*" "*Why can't I ever get this right?*" Those are poisonous questions that our mind is all too happy to answer. These are the sharks in our ocean.

When the lighthouse of awareness shines its light on those parts of our mind, we defeat ourselves. This is the heart of self-sabotage. The words we use against ourselves.

We all have stormy parts of our ocean. Places where the memories of mistakes, bad decisions, and regrets churn like violent, angry seas. Revisiting those hot-spots only reinforces the negative messaging that holds us back. As William Ernest Henley said, "*I am the master of my fate, I am the captain of my soul.*" That doesn't mean we are stuck in the storms of our past. They don't define us, unless we choose to drop anchor there. And why do that? Why spend a waking second of our lives revisiting things that diminish the bright beauty of who we are?

If we were a captain on an actual ship, would we sail where we know a terrible storm is waiting for us? Of course we wouldn't.

We are free to ask ourselves the questions of our choosing. Free to direct the lighthouse to the part of the ocean we want. Even when we're in a tizzy, we can shine the light on something positive. The choice is ours.

"How can I feel better about this situation?" "How can I improve my tennis game?" "How can I lose weight and have fun while doing it?" The ocean is vast. Ask the question. Find the answer. Ask the right questions. Live a more fulfilling life. "How can I fulfill my life's Purpose?"

MENTAL JUNK FOOD

I don't know that I'll ever outgrow funny shirts. A few years ago, I received a shirt as a gift with beautifully written script on the front of it reading, "I will kick your ass in yoga. Namaste." I love that shirt, and wear it regularly when I teach.

I've seen another shirt online that I have yet to buy that reads, "Gluten is the new Al Qaeda." That shirt is clearly yoga teaching material!

It's amazing how much focus has been put on food and nutrition, with more and sometimes contradictory information being released on a consistent basis. Fat is bad. Fat is good. *This* kind of fat is good. GMO vs. Non-GMO.

In the United States, the Food and Drug Administration provides guidelines around the types and amounts of food we should consume on a daily basis. They have established Recommended Dietary Allowances (RDAs) and Adequate Intakes (AIs). On most food packages and containers, we find one value for each nutrient, known as the Daily Value. But where are the guidelines around what we consume mentally?

We can lose hours upon hours of our lives surfing the internet. Remember when internet pages were ad-free? It was pretty easy to digest the information you were looking for. Or when clickbait didn't linger on the sides of a webpage, or down on the bottom, like a thief lurking on the periphery, ready to steal your time at a moment's click? We go to a particular website for specific information, then end up distracted by the mental junk food around that information.

Bruce Springsteen once wrote a song titled, "Fifty-Seven Channels and Nothing on." I think the song needs updating. I haven't counted, but most cable providers now offer a channel selection that seems to range in the hundreds. Channel-surfing has been raised to an art-form and we congratulate ourselves when we find that "gem" of a show that is worthy of our time.

Time is our most precious commodity, and yet we seem all too happy to chuck it over the fence in favor of being entertained. And to what end? We indulge ourselves, then become frustrated when we see the afternoon is gone and the things we wanted to get done still aren't done. The answer we provide ourselves is the reassuring, coldly hollow, "I'll get to it tomorrow." That snapshot becomes one in the portfolio of our lives.

We're gorging ourselves on mental consumption. The problem is, most of what we're ingesting has the nutritional value of mental potato chips. No wonder we find ourselves leading unsatisfying lives.

I recently read a parable attributed to the Cherokee that went like this – a grandfather was talking to his grandson, and he told the grandson that there was a fight going on inside him. The fight was between two wolves. One wolf is evil; it is jealousy, hatred, sorrow, despair, greed, arrogance, self-pity, and guilt. The second wolf is good; it is love, joy, gratitude, sharing, peace, hope, serenity. This fight was taking place within every person, the grandfather said.

The grandson thought about this for a minute, then asked his grandfather, "Which wolf will win?"

The grandfather replied, "The one you feed."

When it comes to understanding our Purpose, the wolves take on a different shape, but they are both equally formidable. One is called Complacency. The other, Commitment. We'll talk about Commitment in a little bit. For now, let's start with Complacency.

Complacency says, wait until tomorrow. It is the enchanting voice of the Greek Sirens, beseeching us to divert from our course, and to rest on yesterday's accomplishments. Every day we listen is a day we crash onto the rocks of procrastination.

Complacency isn't ugly, it's beautiful. It wants us to feel satisfied, to feel content. It doesn't want us to stop doing what we're doing. In that way, it distracts us from pursuing our dreams. From manifesting our Purpose.

Complacency is our internal monologue that says, "this is good enough," "I'm doing better than so-and-so," and "I didn't want that anyway." These things are said with well-meaning intent, but they are really hollow vessels designed for us to pour in our self-pity. When we do that, Complacency smiles. Color us consoled.

Even in writing this book, Complacency greets me every morning. When the alarm goes off at 5 a.m., it tells me that I wrote enough the day prior. I can take a breather. That's part of the reason I started waking up at 4:30 a.m.

Complacency warns us of danger, but millions of years of evolution have caused us to misinterpret the message. Complacency is meant to warn us of stagnation, but we have learned to take it as a message of survival.

The misinterpretation occurs because Complacency is the language of the tribe. The tribe doesn't want risk. The tribe wants safety and security. These factors contribute to survival.

Today, the tribe congregates at cookouts, at the bars, at tailgates. It is at book clubs, and coffees, and luncheons. It is where we commune on what is, and what might have been. This brings us to one of Complacency's greatest ally; Comfort.

Comfort whispers to us that we don't rock the boat. We can enjoy what we have. Comfort, too, is the language of the tribe. The tribe reaffirms that status quo as being okay. We haven't lost anything of consequence. We're safe.

Comfort says, "at least you tried," "you did your best," and "it was a long shot, anyways." These phrases, likes those uttered by Complacency, suggest that failure means it's okay to quit.

Growing up, I enjoyed reading Edgar Rice Burroughs' *Tarzan* series. Neal Adams drew book covers that popped, and the stories always fueled my imagination.

In many ways, each of us is our own Tarzan. Torn between the personal kingdom of our lives, familiar and comfortable, and the other world; that fantastic place which lies beyond the Ocean of Resolve. It is up to us whether we choose to make that voyage.

The voyage is full of unknowns, and like any voyage, if we don't know where we're going, it seems daunting, fraught with peril, and even pointless.

We see that in our everyday lives. We have this surge of energy and enthusiasm to embark upon some new idea or adventure. Something we want to change about ourselves. Our appearance, our recreational activities, or how we otherwise spend our time.

We pledge to ourselves to make the journey. We set sail, feeling confident for a few days. We're taking the steps, taking the action. It's rewarding, invigorating. But then what happens? We look behind us. The shore of what's familiar is still in sight. In fact, it seems closer than ever. We've stopped looking to the horizon, and fall back into our old habits. The *Tide of Comfort* has carried us back to the shores of our familiar.

Success is nothing more than little habits done repeatedly until the desired outcome is achieved, but why does it elude so many of us? Comfort beckons us not to stretch ourselves, instead offering the embrace of the familiar. We want Comfort, we actively seek it, and it is all too happy to oblige.

Think of the child learning to swim. She sits on one of the steps in the water near the shallow end of the swimming pool. Her mother is just beyond arm's reach, beckoning her daughter to make the leap into the water, knowing full well the child is safe.

The child hesitates. The mother is too far. A negotiation begins, where the child wants the mother to move in closer. If the mother fails to acquiesce, the child will cling to the handrail, refusing to make the leap.

For the child, the journey is too dangerous. How many of us tell ourselves that story today?

Think of some of the people who didn't listen to Comfort and Complacency. Imagine if Steve Jobs had said, you know what? I can figure out the iPhone tomorrow. If the Wright brothers had said, it's a beautiful day at the beach. Let's do that whole flying thing next week.

These ideas seem ridiculous to us today. But why? Was the high school educated Steve Jobs smarter than the rest of us? Did Orville and Wilbur have some mystical insight that man could fly? When God was handing out Comfort and Complacency, were they absent?

Together, Complacency and Comfort combine to create the phenomena I call Almost Committed.

ALMOST COMMITTED

Almost Committed in today's culture means, we gave it our best, as if to say the act of trying is somehow commendable and worthy of praise. Almost Committed is having a field day in the United States.

In schools and in sports, we give our children Participation trophies. There are no "winners", or everyone's a winner. We don't want to commit to making distinctions about our children. Imagine how the person who actually finished first feels? Or the person who finished last? Does the last person feel they really did as well as the first? Doubtful. In fact, their enforced "equality" with the first-place winner likely makes them feel worse. Instead of recognizing and lauding those who are gifted in a certain endeavor, we keep them back by making them equal with the rest of the tribe.

We Almost Commit at the altar. Like someone who cautiously wades into the ocean halfway. We find the water's too cold; this isn't what we expected. Instead of "taking the plunge" and fully giving of ourselves, we opt for, "I promise 'till death do us part. Almost."

What happens in every case where the person relents and dives into the water, fully immersing themselves? They surface and say, this feels great. It's not so bad once you're all the way in.

We Almost Commit at work. *Sure, this job is fine for the 30% of the time I'm going to be tuned in to it, and for the 50% of the time I'm actually paying attention. But if they start taking away perks, I'm outta here.* Free soda is, evidently, a big deal.

To sum up where we are at this point – technology, whether it's the TV, our smartphone, or tablet, has us wrapped around its ever-evolving AI finger, providing us with cheap injections of happiness that have us coming back to get our fix. We're overwhelmed with information, and we misinterpret "meaningful thinking" these days as our ability to filter through information, make decisions on the fly, and make it through all the hurdles we face on any given day.

FOUR:
GIMME A DOUBLE-SHOT OF TRUTH, NEAT!

"Truth is like the sun. You can shut it out for a time,
but it ain't goin' away."

~ Elvis Presley

In my coaching practice, people come looking for coaching for a variety of reasons. Some people need career advice, and are uncertain about next steps. Some clients are wrestling with what it is they want to do. They're engaged in a job that isn't rewarding or isn't what they thought it would be, and the wind is quickly leaving their sails. Other people are stuck. Something is holding them back, and that can't see what that is.

Recently I had a client come to me. I've known this person for many years, and had been provided coaching to her on and off over the last decade. She had been in talks with a leader about moving from her current organization to join his team. This move would give her more exposure, more responsibility, and open up future possibilities. All that needed to happen was for him to open a requisition. She would formally apply for the role, and the deal would be done. They continued talking over the course of several months.

At one of their last talks, he informed her he was about to open the requisition. Patiently, she waited, while regularly checking the company's career opportunity website to see if the position had been opened. Nothing. Two weeks later, he called her to let her know he was taking a

WHISKEY AND YOGA: *Find Your Purpose*

position outside the company. She was thrown for a loop. Not only was he not opening the requisition…he wasn't even staying at the company! He did his best to calm her nerves, and told her he would be recommending to his boss that she be his replacement.

This would represent a big jump. She was a manager; his position was that of senior director. Typically, the company didn't allow someone of her grade to apply for a position three grades above hers. Even when the departing director told her that they could figure something out, she was apprehensive.

I told her I was surprised by her anxiety. I'd known her to be someone who was on top of her game. For all the years we'd known one another, she had regularly said she felt she was undervalued by her managers. Now, here was an opportunity for her to make a leap into a role that she could undoubtedly do. This was the chance she had been waiting for.

She finally looked at me and confessed. She was afraid, for the first time in her career, she would get turned down for a job. Her demeanor changed. She recognized that fear was holding her back from seeing this opportunity for what it was. Right then and there, she determined to apply for the position. If she got it, it would be the chance she'd been looking for. If she didn't, she would benefit from the experience of having applied, understand where her opportunities to improve lay, and prepare for the next opportunity. She ended up getting the position.

TRUTH AND CHOICES

I've been married twice and divorced twice, just to keep things balanced. And yet, having a lasting, intimate relationship has long been one of the primary ambitions of my life. I'm a romantic person, but I couldn't find the magic formula to make things work. Yet I had been the one to end both marriages. They were great people, loving partners... what gives?

In my current relationship, we hit it off instantly. When we decided to give a relationship a "go", I wrote her a poem every day for six months. She was great. It was great. This was the best friendship I'd had that had progressed to an intimate relationship.

Then, after about nine months, I started to see the rough spots. They were bubbling to the surface, and the old familiar feeling of needing to punch-out started to surface. I began looking for the door. There were some serious talks, there was gut-wrenching hurt and tears. But I didn't want it to end.

So I stepped back, and asked myself... why was this happening... AGAIN? This was an amazing relationship. We had so much in common. Why did I feel like this huge Meteor of Inevitability was about to crater it? When I really untangled the truth from the lies and stories I told myself over decades, there were two truths that became evident.

The first was, when it came to relationships, I was an asshole. Sure, I could be super-romantic, and even did a good job of doing the little things, like opening doors, putting toothpaste on their toothbrush, and getting flowers. But I could be tremendously selfish by withdrawing or wanting lots of time to myself. That can destabilize a relationship, and without strong lines of communication, it leaves a partner guessing as to where things stand.

The second truth I faced was around "Commitment" and "Committed". If you Google these words, the definitions suggest the words aren't as close together as they might appear. "Commitment" is defined as "an engagement or obligation that restricts freedom of action" while "committed" is defined as "feeling dedication and loyalty to a cause, activity, or job; wholeheartedly dedicated." The second one sounds a lot better than the first. I'm an intelligent guy, at least I'd like to think I am. I've earned two Master's degrees, and been pretty successful over the course of my professional career... what was missing? I hadn't been honest with myself. Almost Committed is really, really, excruciatingly hard. Committed is easy. I had been trying to sell Almost Committed as the full monty. Why? I dug deeper.

Were my dad still alive, my parents would be celebrating their 54th wedding anniversary this summer. They raised two boys in a loving household, and managed to find a way to navigate their tremendous differences. My mom is a chatterbox, my dad could go almost an entire day without saying a word. Mom likes to shop, dad preferred a day on the links. But they found a way, and provided a good example for my brother and me to emulate in terms of a loving, stable relationship. They were committed to one another.

Moving around growing up as a military brat, I hated having to start over. I blamed my dad and the Marine Corps, which is why I didn't want to join the Marines in the first place. I didn't like having to establish new routines and getting familiar with new places. It pained me in a way I couldn't express to have to say goodbye to friends I'd made and start over making new friends. So I learned to set limits on how close I got to people. Even as I wanted to forge close bonds with someone and build a meaningful relationship, I was setting limits. I equated getting too close to someone with pain.

I made a choice to approach relationships in this manner. Right up until I realized I didn't have to make that choice anymore. That was the truth. And that was recognizing a pattern in my life that needed to be disrupted for me to progress. Like the person who wades hip-deep into the ocean, I was afraid of getting cold and wet. What did I need to do? Dive into the damn water. And so, I did.

That's the truth when it comes to our Purpose and succeeding; if we Almost Commit, or we allow ourselves a back-up plan just in case our

Purpose doesn't work out, we will fail. There is no back up plan for life. There is either a life realized, or a life spent in speculation of what might have been.

Our truth can be painful. We hide from ourselves with stories and qualifications we tell ourselves on why things are the way they are. The truth is, things are the way they are because we allow them to be. But we tell ourselves these stories often enough throughout the years that we slowly begin to accept them as the truth.

"TRY HARDER"

What is your truth? What stories have you been telling yourself as part of your consumption habits? Stories that you've been passing off as your truth?

To find our Purpose, we need to understand our truth. We need to take a red pen to our script. We need rewrites! We need to shift our part from a supporting actor in our own story to taking the lead.

If we don't understand our truth, finding our Purpose becomes an elusive and even frustrating exercise. If we're unclear on our truth, we might start to think that our Purpose is what we're currently doing. That may be the case. There are people who love building IT networks. Over the course of my military career, I worked with people who were born to be Marines. If we think we know our Purpose now, and are pursuing it, why aren't we getting the results, the fulfillment that we desire? That can lead us down the exhausting and unrewarding path of trying harder.

Have you ever run a marathon? How about a half-marathon? If you aren't a runner, these distances are daunting. Maybe you'll settle for a 5K. Or maybe running isn't your thing at all, and instead you'll opt for a personal training session at the gym.

How do we prepare ourselves for these events? If we're new to athletics, or to this type of event, we'll jump on the treadmill or the elliptical and go for 20 minutes. Eventually work our way up to 30 minutes. Then 45. Then an hour.

What happens when we do the event? Whether the 5K or the personal training session? We have "just enough" energy to finish. Isn't that amazing? When we finish we say, *I couldn't run another inch.* Or in the case of the personal training session, *I couldn't have gone on a minute longer.*

Of course, neither of these things is "true". We could have run another inch, another foot. We could have gone another mile. If the personal training session lasted an hour, we could have trained for another thirty minutes. We might not have enjoyed it, but we certainly could have done it.

We trick ourselves, don't we? We imagine how much effort the exercise will take, and we prepare to have "just enough" energy to accomplish THAT, and nothing more. And that's exactly what happens. We lie to ourselves to make a truth. This is the rabbit hole that leads to trying harder. This is how we stay "on script" throughout most of our lives.

If we don't accomplish our goal; we don't finish the 5K or have to tap out with fifteen minutes left in the training session, the conclusion we draw is the same. We need to try harder. Trying harder…. i.e., expending more energy and effort will get us closer to our end result, or even over the finish line. The next time, we try harder.

When we try harder, the thing we're looking to accomplish becomes harder to accomplish. If it's the race, the mental barriers we faced before are more prominent. If it's the training session, going the full length of time seems more elusive. Why?

We're grinding our gears. Spinning our wheels when we don't have traction. It becomes an exhausting and futile exercise. Instead of trying harder, we need to change our approach.

Changing our approach can mean anything number of things. How much sleep did we get the night before? What did we eat and drink? Do we have good shoes? Did we stretch?

When I started writing this book, I would get up with the alarm at 5 a.m. After checking the morning headlines, I would grab a cup of coffee or tea and begin writing by 6 a.m. My desk faced the office door. On frequent intervals, the dogs would stroll by. If the door was closed, they would open it. Sometimes the cat would scratch on the closed door until I opened it.

After a few weeks, I realized I wasn't making the progress I wanted. I kept allowing these distractions to occupy my time and get the better of me. After a weekend of reflection, I decided to change my approach.

Now I get up between 4:30-4:40 a.m. I meditate for fifteen minutes, express gratitude for the things I'm thankful for in my life, then hop in a cold shower for a minute. That last part may sound a little nutty, and I should mention I'm writing this in the Spring. Never underestimate the power of a cold shower to get you energized and focused. From there, I dress, go down for a cup of coffee, then grab a seat. I've already been writing this morning for fifteen minutes and it's 5:20 a.m.

I've turned my desk around. Instead of facing the door, it now faces the windows. The dogs and cat are free to come in whenever they feel like. Unless someone hops up into my lap or I get a wet nose rubbing up against my elbow, I hardly notice. So far, it's been very effective in getting me to a place where my writing sessions are better focused.

I'm not trying harder. I've just changed how I approach my writing sessions.

Trying harder then, is a lie. It's a lie that runs rampant in our lives. If we work harder, the thinking goes, we'll get that promotion or that pay bump. If we try harder, our relationship will get better. Because it's a lie, trying harder clouds the truth.

The truth is, we need to change how we look at things, and the things we look at change.

DIGGING IN

I mentioned earlier that in order to find our Purpose, we need to ask the right questions. This seems obvious, but the expanse that opens when asking the next question needs to be accounted for. *What is my Purpose?* We might as well be asking, *why I am here? What's it all about?* But the question does not need to be as daunting as it first appears. We get closer to meat of the question by carving off the fat around it. We do this by asking a few other questions.

Maybe you don't need to ask any more questions, and the answer has already come to you. If that's the case, that is a wonderfully exciting realization to come to. If it hasn't revealed itself, the next question to ask is, *what do I like to do?*

Your first response might be something along the lines of, *I like to drink.* Or, *I like watching TV. I like pilates.* These are easy to dismiss when we hold them up to the original question. Drinking is not a Purpose in life. Watching television, not a Purpose.

In our minds, we can quickly discern there are a host of responses that can be ruled out in the Find My Purpose game. The question gets sharper... *what do I really like to do?*

For me, I love writing. I have always loved writing. In high school, I received national recognition for a short story I wrote. I had poetry published. When I received an unsolicited information package from an art college in Pennsylvania after my sophomore year, I didn't take it seriously. College was two years away at that point. I went to college, thinking I had to put my writing ambitions behind me, so I decided to pursue a major in International Business. Feeling deflated after a semester's worth of courses I wasn't interested in, I went to see a career advisor. She asked me what I really enjoyed doing. I said I enjoyed writing. Presto, I became an English Major.

I was committed to joining the Marine Corps, having earned an NROTC scholarship. When I was commissioned as an officer, I slowly weaned myself off of writing, thinking that Marines didn't write, not creative writing anyway.

But even the Marines couldn't subdue the writer within me. I had the good fortune to work for a battalion commander who painted. I was surprised to find someone who pursued something that most marines laughed at, or at the very least, seemed on the softer side of what people think of when they think of Marines. It was my license to write again. In the fourteen years since working for him, I've written more than five hundred poems.

Over the course of my life, that's what I kept coming back to. Writing. Now? I'm only an unsuccessful writer if I quit. Period. It doesn't matter how much money I make, or how many people read what I've written. If my words reach one person, and that person is inspired to do something more with their life, I've been successful and it's a success from doing something I love to do. What could be better?

BIGGER THAN OURSELVES

Finding our Purpose isn't to say we can't find purpose in the things we do that, ultimately, may not be our Purpose. Participating in the initial landing of Operation RESTORE HOPE in Somalia in 1992 was one of the most purposeful things I've ever done. Why? Because I was participating in something, contributing to something, much bigger than just myself.

That mission…and the Marines' purpose in being there: to provide stability to a war-torn country and to assist with famine relief efforts… was one of the greatest experiences of my life. Though the mission would strain in the months that followed under the weight of the resulting political turmoil our arrival created, on the day we came ashore in Mogadishu, we were greeted with tears and hugs.

What made that day so rewarding, so fulfilling, was that there was no time to be lost in thought. Yes, there was adrenalin surging through each of us, but there was more than that. We all had to be present in the moments as they unfolded around us. Each of us had a role to play in something so much larger than any individual. We were so alive, our senses seemed to be operating in overdrive. We seemed to dissect the cacophony of sounds, between helicopters overhead to radio chatter to people yelling in celebration and honking their horns. In short, we were operating with purpose.

YOUR PURPOSE

Your Purpose is likely very different from mine. Maybe you're mechanical, and you like to build things. Maybe you've wanted to own your own business. Maybe you want to be a wonderful role model for your children or grandchildren. How do you know when you've discovered your life's Purpose?

If we're truthful with ourselves, we know we've hit upon our life's Purpose when we find that one thing that stands out in our minds above everything else. There isn't an alternative. Think about it. If there's something else that comes to mind that means more to us than what we think is our life's Purpose... we haven't yet found our life's Purpose.

If the thing we think is our life's Purpose is something that we have to push ourselves to accomplish, we haven't quite hit the nail on the head. Our life's Purpose shouldn't be something we have to psyche ourselves up for. This isn't like doing that one extra dead lift at the gym, or forcing ourselves to get out of bed without hitting the snooze button seven times. Rather, our life's Purpose is something we're drawn towards. Something we're pulled to, not something we need to push ourselves to achieve.

The next question that comes to mind is, can I have more than one life's Purpose? I would say no. Our Purpose can evolve, or more directly, *our understanding* of our Purpose can evolve.

For instance, if I say my life's Purpose is to write this book, what happens when the book is completed? Have I finished my Purpose in life? Can I clock out? I might realize, writing this book wasn't my life's Purpose. Writing to inspire people... that is my current understanding of my life's Purpose. And it will continue to evolve. I may boil it down to "Inspiring People" is my life's Purpose. Whether through writing, coaching, or public speaking, I am pursuing my Purpose in life.

Fundamentally, I believe there are two elements everyone's Purpose contains: giving and creating.

Our Purpose must contain an element of giving. That's what made being in Somalia such a rewarding experience. When we were providing security as much-needed food got delivered to distribution centers across the city, we were helping people stay alive. We can't say, "*my Purpose in life is to make millions of dollars, or to be super-rich.*" That sounds great, but what are you going to give in order to become super wealthy? Even the lottery requires the purchase of a ticket.

Our Purpose must contain an element of creating. That IS our Purpose. To create. How it manifests itself in each of us is different. That is our gift. We can create something tangible such as a book, a piece of art, or a house. Or we can create something intangible, like hope. Robin Williams created joy. Steve Jobs created awe. He also created many tangible objects that changed the world. We see a veteran whose body has been shattered by war. Their Purpose in life is to demonstrate the power of the human spirit. They create inspiration.

Henry Ford created a new kind of engine. Thomas Edison created the light bulb. Mahatma Gandhi created a civil rights movement which brought India its independence. The list of creators throughout human history is fantastic. These were people who realized and lived their Purpose.

What is your Purpose? When you understand your Purpose, how do you begin changing your life to start realizing it? It starts with the decisions we make.

FIVE:

DECISIONS ON THE ROCKS

*"If the fate of the universe was decided in a single moment
at the instant of the Big Bang,
that was the most creative moment of all."*

~ Deepak Chopra

The two months I spent in Somalia were part of a larger six-month deployment spent aboard U.S. Navy ships as part of a western Pacific deployment. Life at sea is both nostalgic and tedious. And that's if you're a Marine. For the Navy, the ship is on the move, day and night. As a Marine officer, I quickly realized there are only so many classes we can teach to the Marines before they become redundant. The weapons aren't being fired, so don't need cleaning. Once a month, we might have a live-fire off the back of the ship. But that's a few hours' worth of cleaning, tops.

I saw my life back in San Diego in a fishbowl. All the things I enjoyed, all the things I hated, were "back there". I thought about this, and told myself I was going to make changes. To make better decisions. I saw how I wanted my life to be, and saw what I needed to change it to get it there. I remember sharing this thought at one point with one of the infantry company commanders. This was his third cruise.

He said you always see your life for what it is, and what you want it to be. You tell yourself you're going to change it, but then when you get back home, you fall into the same trappings and habits you had before. He wasn't bitter when he said it. Just matter-of-factly. I didn't walk away from the conversation disgruntled. We weren't going to be home anytime soon, so what did it matter?

Turns out he was right. I got back to San Diego in April of 1993 with a mental list of things I wanted to change. After a few weeks, I was doing the same things I'd done before I'd left.

DECISIONS, DECISIONS

We make decisions on a minute-by-minute basis, every day of our lives. What we're having for lunch... do I have enough time to go to the store... do we continue with this project or give it the axe?

To make an informed decision, we gather information, assess the resolutions available to us, and (hopefully) choose the resolution that will bring about the desired result. It's exhausting. In fact, we love when we don't have to make decisions. We pass it off... *you decide what we're doing tonight, what we're having for dinner. I don't care.*

It's like we have a finite number of good decisions allotted to us every day. Once those good decisions are all used up, all bets are off.

Decision-making can make us angry, and lead to us making bad decisions. If the kids are in the backseat arguing incessantly, in a huff we decide to skip the grocery store, even though we know we need to go. They can settle for leftovers tonight, and they deserve it after all this screaming. We get in a fight with our spouse and decide to have a drink to take the edge off our anger, or to dull the pain. When we've emptied the shelves of good decision-making, impulse takes over. We even KNOW we're making bad decisions, but instead of caring, prefer to deal with the consequences, whatever they end up being.

Alternatively, we have the option of doing nothing. It's the easiest decision to make. Can't decide which weekend chore to start first? Let's sit on the couch for an hour with the boob-tube. It's still a decision.

The decisions we make change over time. When we're younger, we make hasty and impulsive and rash decisions. When these lead to mistakes, or end up being bad decisions, we take away lessons from these experiences to shape future decisions.

Some of us do a better job of this than others. I made bad decisions for longer than I intended. At times, I felt like I'd earned a third Master's degree; this one, in bad decision-making.

The key to stopping bad decision-making is to learn from the decisions we've made. If we keep doing the same thing we've been doing but expect a different outcome... isn't that the definition of insanity?

As we grow older, we should be making better decisions. We become risk averse and, generally speaking, our decision-making reflects this. We err on the side of caution with our decisions.

From an evolutionary standpoint, we have evolved to put our safety and survival at the top of our priority list. This guides our decision-making to preserve the sense of comfort we've created for ourselves. The story may have different settings and different supporting actors, but our script is centered around comfort.

PUSHING THROUGH IMPOSSIBILITY

Of the big four main military branches, the Marine Corps leads the way in bad-assery. This is to say that the basic training for both officers and enlisted Marines pushes individuals into the realm of being uncomfortable better than the other branches. I'm within my rights in saying this, having attended Marine Corps Officers Candidate School, The Basic School (the six-month officer training all Marine officers undergo before pursuing their field of specialty... also known as TBS or The Big Suck), and Army Officers Basic Artillery School, which serves as the initial officer training for Army second lieutenants pursuing an artillery specialty. Additionally, I spent a tour on the drill fields of Parris Island, South Carolina training Marine recruits, and had the opportunity to observe Army enlisted basic training. The Navy drives ships, and the Air Force flies planes, but their basic training doesn't compare to the Army or the Marine Corps.

Within each branch, there are deeper, elite levels of bad-assery. The Navy has the SEALs; the Army, Green Berets; the Air Force, Combat Controllers; the Marines, Recon. I don't attribute Delta Force to any one branch, as my understanding is Delta recruits from all the branches of service. I can't tell you whether that's true or not. If I told you, I'd have to kill you.

The equation of bad-assery is simple: discomfort plus duration. How long can you deal with being cold? How much shivering are you willing to put up with? How long will you go without sleep? Yes, I understand your muscles are aching from carrying this telephone pole, but your team has three hundred meters to go.

To the person who has never traveled down this route, understanding what this looks like is most accessible in watching videos of candidates undergoing BUDS training, or Basic Underwater Demolition/SEAL training. How uncomfortable does it get? They have a "drown-proofing" test for one. Candidates spend excessive amounts of time in the chilly waters off of

Coronado Island. Everyone's lips are purple, everyone's teeth are chattering. Hypothermia becomes a familiar friend. Not for you? No biggie. Ring the bell that signals you're tossing in the towel. Being a SEAL isn't for lots of people.

Something amazing happens when we push ourselves, or are pushed, past our self-perceived limits. The world we live in changes. Something we thought was impossible or unattainable suddenly isn't.

SEEKING DISCOMFORT

One of the most physically challenging trials of Marine Corps Officer Candidate School (OCS) was the Battle Fitness Test, or BFT. The test was a run wearing combat boots across nine miles in the woods of Quantico, Virginia on a broiling day the last week in June. Sprinkled along the course were obstacles we would have to negotiate. We each carried two canteens and our M16A2 rifles. The BFT was a graduation requirement; there was no make-up if it was raining, or the day was too hot.

The Marines warn of the acceptable level of outdoor activity during hot summer days using a system of flags flying at various points aboard the base. Green meant it was okay to do normal outdoor training, yellow meant to exercise caution, red meant severely limit outdoor training. The day we ran the flag was black. No outdoor training. No make-ups. We ran the course.

I had been mentally preparing myself for the BFT for weeks. Prior to arriving at OCS, I'd run eleven miles in humid Georgia. My thinking was, if I could do that, the BFT would be easier. I never questioned IF I could do it. I just wondered how much it was going to suck.

By that point in training, our platoon of fifty had lost ten candidates. A few had been medically injured, and would recycle with another OCS class later that summer, or have to wait until the next year. Some had been given the boot because they weren't what the Marine Corps was looking for from its officers.

While running the BFT, our platoon commander got lost and we ended up running three extra miles. Of the forty candidates who started the BFT that morning, thirteen finished. Someone went into a coma from heat stroke. They found him on the side of the trail, coughing up blood. Someone else fractured their ankle. Another candidate had fractured a thigh.

I was one of the thirteen. I wasn't in better shape than any of those who fell out, or those that stopped to help the injured. I knew it would be uncomfortable, and I was prepared.

THE ART OF UNCOMFORT

I am not suggesting we have to get THAT uncomfortable, but I am saying that discomfort is a companion we need to get close to. I call it the Art of Uncomfort. Uncomfort is going without the Comfort that we find so readily to nurse us in our Complacency.

Uncomfort brings us in to the present moment. It forces us to engage our senses, to assess what is and what isn't. What matters and what doesn't.

Uncomfort is both engaging and draining, because it forces us to think. It encroaches on our senses, and erodes the time in which we're daydreaming.

Uncomfort screams "We're not done yet," "Don't give up" and "Keep going". It is the Marine drill instructor of your soul.

How do we apply Uncomfort? Change starts from within. Other people won't change you. Institutions won't change you. They may provide you with a blue print for change, they may draw something out from you that you didn't know existed. But you are the captain of your ship. It's up to you, and the decisions you make. To shake ourselves away from our comfort zone, we have to decide in favor of Uncomfort. Uncomfort means not hitting the snooze button. It is the bridge between the living the life you expect and living the life you want.

Uncomfort is the bridge we must cross to realize our Purpose.

HABITS AND EMOTIONS

With our decisions, we create habits and then patterns in our lives. We do this somewhat consciously so that we have less decisions to make. I'm going to the gym at 6 p.m. On Thursdays I do yoga. We have our team meeting the third Wednesday of every month. As our lives become a reflection of our decisions and actions, our lives also become a reflection of our habits.

Andrew Stanton, who wrote the *Toy Story* movies at Pixar once said, "*We all fall into our routines, our habits, our ruts. They're used quite often, consciously or unconsciously, to avoid living, to avoid doing the messy part of having relationships with other people, of dealing with a person next to us. That's why we can all be in a room on our cell phones and not have to deal with one another.*" When we want to change, we need to start by looking at the habits we've formed. We can't inject any more time into a day, so we need to look at our choices and our decisions.

For years, I listened to a famous radio personality on my drive in to the office every morning. It was a chance for me to start thinking about my day, thinking about what I wanted to accomplish. Instead, I used it to be entertained.

My morning routine was pretty typical. I would wake up, throw on *Sportscenter* to get caught up on scores and highlights I'd missed from the previous day while eating breakfast. During this time, I would check and answer email on my phone. After thirty minutes of updates, I'd turn off the television and get all my things together to head in to the office. Once in my car, the radio was tuned to my favorite morning radio show. My commute was anywhere from ten to fifteen minutes depending on traffic. Thanks to satellite radio, if I missed part of the broadcast in the morning, it ran in a loop, and I could catch more of his show on my drive home.

Some time back, I changed this. At first, it was hard. I enjoyed the radio show. It was an easy and automatic part of my morning. I liked hearing about the antics of the host and his staff and guests. But I wanted to use that time in a more meaningful way. Instead of listening to something that was entertaining, I started listening to things that were educational and informative. I started listening to podcasts and audiobooks. I started engaging my brain, thinking about what my schedule for the day looked like. What I wanted to get done. I embraced the Art of Uncomfort to make this change in my life.

In order to do this, I had to be present. Some days, I would get in the car and start driving to the office. After five minutes, I'd realize that I hadn't turned off the radio show. I hadn't been present and had just relied on an old habit.

In order to change a habit, we need to give the habit our attention. We need to understand the habit for what it is, and why we want to change it. Moreover, we need to replace it with a new decision that we intend on making a habit.

How many times have we said we DON'T want to do something, only to keep coming back to it time and time again? If we're familiar with the Law of Attraction, we know that focusing on not wanting something is no better than focusing on wanting it. We have to replace it and remove it from our minds. We can increase the success and speed with which we make this change by injecting emotion into the equation.

When we assign emotion to the change, we lay the groundwork for a meaningful and lasting change. Let me give you an example on the importance emotion plays in facilitating change.

If we work together, and I come by your office. It's mid-day. I stroll in to your office, lean up against the wall. I wait for you to give me your attention. When I have it, I casually say to you, almost in a whisper, "you know... there's a fire... pretty good-sized fire in the break room. You may want to consider evacuating." What will your reaction be? You might ask me if I'm joking; my demeanor suggests it isn't a big deal. The fact that I'm whispering stands in stark contrast to the message I'm relaying. You resolve it in your mind that I am joking, and go back to what you were doing.

On the other hand, if I come running in to your office, slam my fist against the wall to get your attention, then scream at you, "THERE IS A

MASSIVE FIRE IN THE BREAK ROOM! LEAVE YOUR LAPTOP AND GET OUT OF THE BUILDING NOW." Your reaction will be dramatically different. My emotional state influenced a change in you.

When we were younger, what did we do before we went out for a big basketball or football game? We pumped ourselves up. We brought emotion into the mix. We did so to get us focused, to get energized. To give our best to the task at hand. Today, we may do something similar before we give a presentation. The level of energy may not be exactly the same, but the intention is there.

Need any more examples? Think of any military movie, TV show, or documentary you've seen that shows military drill instructors at work. Emotion equals change. These are examples of external influence to change our emotional state, but we can do the same thing by ourselves. Ever get amped up before you played a game? How about psyching yourself up before you have to give a presentation, or before you're speaking in front of an audience? Emoting works.

When we want to make a change in our lives, we can't whisper it. If we want it to last, we have to scream it. We need energy. Enthusiasm. We need passion. Notice, I'm not saying we need to try harder. Passion towards something isn't the same as how we approach it. Passion is invigorating and engaging. Trying harder is frustrating and exasperating. Passion helps to lessen the resistance to Uncomfort.

YOUR PURPOSE SHERPA

When we look at our habits, we need to look at our consumption habits. What are we consuming mentally? Earlier I talked the attention given to healthy eating habits. Now, let's talk in greater depth about mental consumption.

You've probably heard phrases like, *The Body is a Temple*, or *If you want a Ferrari body, you can't feed it low-octane fuel*. The same is true for our minds. Our mind is a temple. The most important of temples. And if you want a Ferrari mind, you can't feed it low-octane information.

Earlier, I also talked about if I want to be a millionaire, I need to think like a millionaire. If I wanted to be a movie director, I needed to think like a movie director. There's another saying you may have heard that pertains to the body and exercise; if you want to get stronger, work out with people stronger than you. The thinking is, we will workout harder and with more enthusiasm if our training partner is stronger than we are.

When we understand our Purpose, the odds are we aren't yet a master of that field of practice. If we were, we would probably have capitalized on our Purpose some time ago. In the same way we want to workout with someone stronger than us, when it comes to our Purpose we need to look for people who have successfully gone down a similar path. We need a Purpose Sherpa, or Sherpas.

In other words, if I want to be an investor, do I want to learn from someone like Warren Buffett, or Bernie Madoff, the fraudster behind the largest Ponzi scheme in U.S. history? If I want to be a football coach, do I find out what I can from someone like Bill Belichek. Or do I find the college football coach whose team hasn't won a game the past three seasons?

Some of the most accomplished people in all of human history are living in our present time. Some have written books, in an effort to pass on their wisdom and share some of their insights. That is the kind of information we should look to add to our consumption diet.

For all the woes technology has given us with regard to information overload, there's an interesting benefit of technology that's come to light recently. If you spend any time on YouTube, chances are you've seen one. These are video infomercials of the X-Entrepreneurs as I call them. This is the next generation of entrepreneurs, carving a path through a dynamic business world that is still coming of age. The infomercials are really stepping-stones into their programs where, for a price, you can glean from them their best practices and habits that have led them to current financial success they enjoy. For some people, someone in their 30's discussing how they made their millions may be more relatable than someone like Warren Buffett. Tai Lopez is my favorite. He seems very relatable, has enjoyed fantastic success, and has a keen understanding of how to market himself.

If we're unsure of what our Purpose is, there are guides to lead us down the path of understanding and finding our Purpose. Napoleon Hill's *Think and Grow Rich* is a great place to start. After watching a video online of Bob Proctor explaining the interconnection between the conscious mind, the subconscious mind and the body, I picked up a copy of *Think and Grow Rich*. Reading that book sent me on the path of writing this book.

If my Purpose and passion is around real estate, pursuing a program or expertise around flipping houses makes sense. If my Purpose is writing and inspiring people, the flipping houses program doesn't seem like a good fit. There are numerous classes online now, taught by "Masters" who can help guide us down our respective paths.

When we understand our Purpose, we can begin making decisions that revolve around realizing that Purpose. Equipped with this focused decision-making, we begin to structure our lives around Purpose. This brings greater satisfaction to our everyday living.

PART TWO:
YOGA

SIX:

OM-M-G, YOU NEED A PLAN

*"Sutra 32: The practice of concentration on a single object is
the best way to prevent obstacles and their accompaniments."*

~ Sri Patanjali, The Yoga Sutras of Patanjali

The Yoga Sutras of Patanjali are widely considered to be the author-itative text on yoga. The following quote from him, written some sixteen hundred years ago, provides an insight on the revelation of Purpose:

*"When you are inspired by some great purpose, some extraordinary
project, all your thoughts break their bonds: your mind transcends
limitation, your consciousness expands in every direction, and you
find yourself in a new, great and wonderful world. Dormant forces,
faculties and talents become alive, and you discover yourself to be a
greater person by far than you ever dreamed yourself to be."*

The making of a plan sounds painful. It brings to mind writing things down, assigning milestones, creating checklists… things that can be tedious and not all that fun. Fortunately, that's not the type of plan I'm talking about. In fact, the plan I'm talking about is quite different from that.

I didn't have a plan for becoming a yoga instructor. I knew I liked yoga, and I liked the idea of teaching something I liked to others. I took that idea, that vision, and came up with a plan. It wasn't exact. It wasn't perfect. I didn't write anything down. There was no "be a yoga instructor by this date" stuck on the refrigerator door. I had a vision. The plan took care of itself. Now, I have had a regular teaching practice for eight of the last ten years.

The vision is more important than the plan. The plan can change; the vision shouldn't. It's like riding a motorcycle. Before I bought my last Harley Davidson, I attended a motorcycle safety course offered by my local dealer. It had been twenty years since I'd last ridden, and I knew a refresher would serve me well.

In the class, one of the key lessons they offered was this; the bike will go where you're looking. If you're looking at a tree, you're going to hit the tree. When you're making a slow turn and the bike starts to lean with the turn, look where you want to go. If you look down, you're going to drop the bike or at the very least need to put a foot down.

THE LAW

I heard a story of a teenage physicist who was asked what he thought God was. He replied that he thought God preceded the Big Bang. Because God wanted knowledge, It made Itself into stars and galaxies. It became planets and black holes. And then It became life.

I found the story compelling because it's a scientist giving his view on God, and the view he gives is in line with the Hindu notion that God is in every atom. If this idea is true, it helps to explain how and why the Law of Attraction works.

Napoleon Hill wrote the first best-seller on the Law of Attraction with his 1937 book, *Think and Grow Rich*. Before that, Wallace Wattles wrote in 1910 in *The Science of Getting Rich*:

> *"It is the natural and inherent impulse of life to seek to live more; it is the nature of intelligence to enlarge itself, and of consciousness to seek to extend its boundaries and find fuller expression. The universe of forms has been made by Formless Living Substance, throwing itself into form in order to express itself more fully."*

Wattles went on to say that this Formless Living Substance was at the command of men and women, providing they think and act in a Certain Way. The "Certain Way" he was referring to was the Law of Attraction.

The leading authors on the Law of Attraction agree that it has been around since man first thought. Before Hill and Wattles, Helena Blavatsky first used the term "The Law of Attraction" in her 1877 book, *Isis Unveiled*.

If we revisit historical quotes and look at them through the lens of the Law of Attraction, we see evidence of its presence two thousand years ago. In the King James Version of the Bible, Jesus says, *"Ask, and ye shall receive; seek, and ye shall find; knock, and it shall be opened unto you."*

Nor is this historical understanding of the Law of Attraction limited to Western Civilization. Buddha said, "*All that we are is a result of what we have thought.*"

James Allen expanded on Buddha's notion in his book, *As a Man Thinketh.* He says:

> *A man's mind is like a garden, it may be intelligently cultivated or allowed to run wild; but whether cultivated or neglected, it must, and will bring forth. If no useful seeds are put into it, then an abundance of useless weed-seeds will fall therein, and will continue to produce their kind.*

The Law is absolute. Given this fact, the Law is a good tool to understand and take with us in the formulation of our plan.

OVER-RELIANCE ON A PLAN

I was building something with my significant other's six-year-old daughter recently. She wanted to build a bridge out of these little sticks that were a blend of Lincoln logs and Legos. She went on to explain to me how we connected the pieces together by interlocking sections at the ends of each piece. She then proceeded to go on a connecting frenzy, adding piece after piece to her construction. When she was finished, she had something that resembled a warped snowflake. I asked her what happened to her bridge. She said she wasn't sure. I suggested to her, that perhaps she'd gotten so caught up in connecting pieces, she lost sight of what she was building. She looked at me and smiled as we proceeded to take the snowflake apart and start over.

If we rely too much on a plan, our focus shifts from the vision of what we're trying to accomplish to ensuring we're addressing all the milestones within our plan. Our plan becomes this prescriptive obligation where we're checking boxes. The plan needs to support our vision, not weigh it down.

DEFINE YOUR PURPOSE

Here, in broad brushstrokes, is the plan I propose to you:

1. Define your Purpose

What is your Purpose? The questions we ask ourselves matter, and this is one of the most important questions to ask and to answer. Here, we aren't talking about your purpose for reading this book, or the purpose of you working at your job. We're talking about your Purpose in life. Approach this question from different angles to really come to an understanding. Why are you here on the planet? How can you make the greatest impact with your life? What unique gift do you have to offer to the world?

Once you have your Purpose identified, write it down. On paper. In ink. The simple act of writing your Purpose down helps focus your mind, your energy, your soul towards embracing this as your reality. When you write it down, you engage your long-term memory. Ever have a bright idea you decided to write down? It's accessible all day. Ever write down a "to-do" list and remember everything on it, even after you've left it on the kitchen counter? That's the power of writing things down.

What does this look like? Perhaps it's something like this – "*My DEFINITE PURPOSE in life is to energize people with my passion, inspire them to realize their dreams. I am unrelenting in my pursuit of realizing my life's Purpose, and I know I am the Master of my soul and the Captain of my fate. I bring unbridled enthusiasm, my heart, my sweat, and my courage to everyday live life to the fullest, to BE the inspiration for people across the world. I am a champion. I am a warrior, and I will never surrender in pursuing my Purpose.*"

Maybe it's something more concrete. "*My ONE CHIEF AIM in life is to entertain people with my stories by writing books that inspire, encourage, and fascinate readers across the world. I eagerly write every day stories that are captivating and engaging. I write stories that matter! I draw from the rich abundance of life to create intriguing characters, invigorating storylines that beautifully come together into novels that people want to read. I harness my power, my creativity and my subconscious mind to become the best writer I can possibly be, and I commit myself to this life NOW."*

These are just two examples. The first one might be someone who is a life coach, a public speaker or even some kind of sport's coach. The second is an author. Write an affirmation or Purpose Contract that suits your Purpose. It can be as long or as short as you want. But the more clearly you articulate what it is, the more you give your mind something to focus on. Sign your name at the end of your Purpose.

Once you've written it down, read it out loud. Every day. Read it on the days you feel sick. On the days you wake up late and are rushed. Read it with emotion. Engage your body and your mind. Remember, thought is energy. When you're passionate about something, your body chemistry changes. In addition to reading it out loud daily, you should write it down several times. This locks it in to your subconscious mind. Cements it.

Reading it aloud every day is an affirmation and a reminder of why you're here. Embrace this realization. Fulfill your Purpose.

2. Visualize your Purpose realized

Have you heard of visualization? Of Olympic athletes visualizing a successful pole vault, or winning the gold medal because they visualized it? This is Law of Attraction 101. If you're unfamiliar with the Law of Attraction, the law says that whatever you focus your thoughts on, you attract into your life. If your thoughts are negative, negativity will come in to your life. If positive thoughts dominate, positivity will follow you.

If you have your Purpose already, visualize it. Put the book down, close your eyes, and visualize your Purpose for anywhere from thirty seconds to a minute. Don't think about accomplishing your Purpose, about striving to bring it about. Think about it as being accomplished. Let's say you want to help people find their dream home, and you want to become a real estate guru. Visualize that you are. How does that feel? Are your clients grateful for helping them find a home they love and can afford? How much commission are you making? Are you flipping houses? How much is that worth? Visualize having that exact amount. How does that feel?

The more focus and clarity you can bring to your Purpose and to understanding what you want, the more the Law of Attraction works for you. When you visualize your Purpose realized, you attract accomplishing your Purpose into your life. This may seem like a silly point but think about this for a moment. "Trying to do something" and "doing something" are not the same thing. Almost Committed and Committed... not the same thing. Being a movie nut, it takes me back to the immortal words of Yoda from *The Empire Strikes Back*, and something I regularly tell my yoga students – *Do or do not. There is no try.*

There are three key elements you should look to include when you visualize your Purpose: your Purpose, what you want in return, and when you want it.

What do you want in return for sharing your Purpose with the world? I assume, unless you're channeling your inner Mother Theresa, you want money. But how much money do you want? Again, I assume you want enough where you can quit your current job, gain financial freedom, and live the life you've always imagined. How much money will that take? The more specific a dollar figure you bring to mind, the more easily the Law of Attraction will bring that in to your life.

If you say, "I want more money than I can imagine," that isn't very specific. On the other hand if you say, "I want five million dollars" or "I want fifty thousand dollars a month," those are more specific and the Law of Attraction will work with you. When you step back and think about it, this all makes sense. How would you plan for more money than you could imagine? It isn't really a tangible goal. The other two are.

Finally, when do you want to have realized your Purpose? Much like any goal in life, our thoughts shift when we have a date around which to focus. This needs to be realistic. If you say, "I want to be a real estate mogul and make ten million dollars by this weekend," but have never bought or sold a house, don't have a real estate license, and have planned a weekend trip to the beach, odds are you aren't going to be a real estate mogul before next Monday. When you set a date, it needs to be a date that you believe is achievable. If there is a monetary aspect to realizing your Purpose, write this down as well. In the second example I provided, the author's Purpose, we can speculate that there is a monetary value the author has in mind for the completion and publication of their next novel. That would be written as, "I have a two million dollar book contract for my next book, which I will complete by (insert date here)." Notice here, I didn't write in terms of *wanting* the two million dollar contract, but in terms of *having* it.

The Law of Attraction is universal and absolute. Smarter people than I have written in detail about the Law. One thing to be mindful of is regarding using the Law. Focusing on not wanting something in your life is the same as focusing on wanting it – "It" is still the object of your focus. I touched on this earlier, but it's worth mentioning again. If your focus is around money, and your thoughts are centered on the idea, "I don't want to be broke," that's not good. The Law will keep coming back to the object that you're focused on. In this case, it's being broke. It's better to focus on wanting something in the positive sense, rather than not wanting something in the negative sense. Use the Law wisely.

3. Change your decisions to support your Purpose.

This is the meat and potatoes of changing your life. Your thoughts and actions, your decisions and choices, have led you to where you are in your life today. With your Purpose now in hand, your decisions need to change to support the realization of that Purpose. New habits need to be formed. Your brain needs to be rewired to accomplish this.

This can sound daunting at first, especially when viewed in the light of past experiences. It's that gym membership that isn't getting used, or that pledge to quit eating potato chips that isn't being honored. How is this time different?

Simple. This is your life's Purpose. The reason you're on the planet. Think about how empowering that is. Some people go their entire lives, lives of 60, 70, maybe even 100 years, and don't come to understand their life's Purpose. Coming to understand your life's Purpose means you've run out of excuses. This becomes the launching point for massive change.

And yet, it can start very simply by writing down what your Purpose is, what you want in return for it, and the date you want it realized. Putting Purpose to pen and paper shows you're committed. To strengthen that commitment, read aloud your Purpose daily. I read mine in the morning before I start writing. At frequent intervals, I write it down, again and again.

This single decision – writing down this affirmation of who you are and why you're on the planet – has staggering implications. Your mind will begin to shift immediately towards grappling with your Purpose. You will start to think about your Purpose more and more.

As this happens, your decision-making will start to change. Your decisions will be anchored around your Purpose. Things that are a part of your life that aren't important to the realization of your Purpose will become less important. The decision of writing down your Purpose, coupled with the habit of reading it aloud daily becomes ground zero for orchestrating massive change in your life.

4. Become Purposefully Obsessed

Your Purpose isn't going to happen without your attention being given to it. It's the opposite of the old adage, "*A watched pot never boils*"... *an un-minded Purpose never comes to fruition.*" You need to keep your Purpose at the forefront of your thoughts. Your Purpose becomes the point on the horizon towards which your ship is sailing. Purposeful Obsession is the galvanizing force that keeps your thoughts and actions centered around your Purpose.

A critical component of Purposeful Obsession is having absolute faith and conviction that your Purpose will be realized. When we're younger, we don't always believe in ourselves. We look for reassurance from our parents, family, and close friends. For some of us, we never get over that self-doubt. But if you don't believe in your Purpose, why will anyone else?

Faith is instrumental in the realization of your Purpose. The stories you tell yourself throughout your life may or may not always be true. It's the script. It's living up to other people's expectations. But an interesting thing happens when you realize your Purpose. Your words become truer than they have ever been. That seems strange, doesn't it? It's true. Think about it.

You go through life, trying to make sense of things. You tell yourself things to make you feel better about circumstances, about life in general. They may be partial truths, or they may not have a shred of truth to them. Gradually, you accept them as true.

When you realize your life's Purpose, the universe seems to come into alignment. Everything "fits." You see more clearly than you ever have before. The sharpness you have in your mind translates to the "truth" coming out in your words. You'll know this when it happens. Have complete trust that your Purpose will be realized, and it will be.

If this is your life's Purpose, how can you possibly not accomplish it? By failing? Henry Ford once said, *"Failure is simply the opportunity to begin again, this time more intelligently."* In other words, failure and quitting are not the same thing. We fear failure, but failure is our best teacher. This was a man who spent more than a year telling engineers to build a V-8 engine block. Every time he told them, they told him it was impossible. And yet, Henry Ford saw his relatively inexpensive V-8 engine come into existence.

He didn't have a plan, but the "plan" ultimately revealed itself, and the impossible became possible. Henry Ford had a vision and the conviction to see his vision realized.

Many people shy away from yoga, thinking it's too hard. They say, *"I'm not that flexible. I can't even touch my toes."* Lots of people can't touch their toes when they start. But with perseverance and dedication, it happens. And it doesn't take a year.

Some people take the same approach when it comes to their Purpose. They think it will be too hard, or will take too long. That they don't have the money, the knowledge, or the time. So they talk themselves out of it, then can't understand why their life isn't more fulfilling. It's like not buying a lottery ticket, then getting upset when you don't win.

Your Purpose is your lottery ticket. And if you believe in your Purpose, you're *guaranteed* to win.

5. Stay positive and grateful

We've created a world of instant gratification. A vast amount of information is available at our fingertips. If we see something we want and can afford, it can be delivered to our doorstep within hours.

Your Purpose could be realized in a matter of days, weeks, even months. Or it could take a year, or more. It's crucial that you stay upbeat. There are plenty of cheap dopamine fixes available to you, but nothing is more fulfilling than realizing your life's Purpose.

It doesn't sound very positive, but think of what you want people to say at your funeral. Do you want them to say, *"he had dreams that he gave up on"* or *"he died doing what he loved."* Is it more fulfilling to live a life where you played it safe right up until you died, or daring to dream big to leave your mark on the world? I vote the latter.

At the end of my yoga class when students are coming out of their savasana, I suggest to them they take a few breaths in silence, offering gratitude for their practice. Being grateful as our Purpose manifests itself is important.

When we have positive thoughts and thoughts of gratitude, we bring more positivity and more reasons to be grateful into our lives.

That's the plan. Was it what you expected? Does it sound "touchy-feely" as we used to say in the Marines when anything came up that bordered on our sense of compassion? How we think is of paramount importance to realizing our Purpose.

SEVEN:

DHYANA CHECK OUT MY ASANA?

*"The cosmos is within us. We are all made of star-stuff.
We are a way for the universe to know itself."*

~ Carl Sagan

As I started down the path of becoming a yoga teacher, I wasn't the best student. I discovered yoga as I was leaving active duty with the Marines. The only reason I had bothered looking in to it was I'd read an article in a sports magazine about NFL players using it to strengthen their midsections. Football players were manly. The Marines were manly. Yoga did not seem manly, but if football players were doing it, that was good enough for me.

Yoga was super touchy-feely, and the culture was one hundred and eighty degrees out from what I'd known in the Marine Corps. To hear tree-hugging teachers talk about how we're all connected to some mystical source seemed outlandish. The one saving grace to yoga for me was, it had a thread that seemed connected to the code of the Samurai, or Bushido. I spent three years as a kid living in Japan, and learned about the code of the samurai, which spoke of loyalty, courage, and honor... things I'd learned in the Marines. The code also spoke of compassion, and an appreciation and respect for life. Those were present in the yoga community, and in the instructors I learned from.

But universal oneness? At the time, I was unconvinced. After all, we're living in a material world. Now, thanks to science and quantum physics, I have a different view.

Let's get quantum for a second, shall we? Forget the world you think you know. See the world the way Neo saw the Matrix, with just a slight variation. Instead of seeing the world as nothing more than computer code, see the world for what it is. The world is a massive ocean of atoms. An almost infinite number of atoms arranged into different objects. Even space, with its vast emptiness, has wisps of hydrogen gas… atoms that seemingly connect the atoms on earth to the planets and stars. Here on earth, some atoms form trees, other come together to form clouds. Some arrange and form plants, some animals. Some form us.

Life is pretty spectacular from this vantage point. Within the collection of atoms that is each human, a sentient being exists. We are able to feel, perceive, and experience the world around us. We do this subjectively, meaning your experience, perception, and feeling is different from mine.

Animals are said to be sentient, though there is an ongoing debate on the level of that sentience. At present, scientists are wrestling with whether Artificial Intelligence will be sentient, and whether or not we'll ever be able to determine A.I. sentience.

Since we know atoms are constantly moving, we can imagine they are constantly bouncing against one another. We identify this as vibration. The desk we work from, the car we drive… all vibrating. All of us, despite how solidly we seem to be built, are vibrating.

Is our vibration always the same? We know our office desk isn't sentient; it's just a desk made of wood, or particle board and panels. It doesn't have ambitions, it doesn't feel anything. With that understanding, we can assume the desk vibrates at the same frequency, or within a narrow frequency band.

When we're angry, are we vibrating at a different frequency? Our pulse is accelerated, our temple is pounding. Our eyes may bulge with our increased blood pressure. We react with hostility to the world around us – a sunny day is too hot, a rainy day is miserable, traffic sucks. Our perception has changed based on our emotional condition. What about when we're happy?

When we're completely happy, we feel great. We have no aches or pains, and a smile dances across our face. We're not even aware of our blood pressure. We feel in harmony with the world, even if we don't consciously acknowledge it. A sunny day is amazing, a rainy day is bringing nourishment to our lawn and garden, and traffic is flowing. Here too, our feelings have shaped how we're experiencing the world in which we live.

If we're a collection of atoms operating in a world of atoms, we can say the arrangement of atoms that is "us" is operating at a different frequency in each of the two above-mentioned cases. If that's true, it stands to reason we should want to stay in the happiness end of the frequency spectrum more than the angry end.

PERCEPTION AND REALITY

Have you seen the video online about the scientist and the water experiment? Dr. Masaru Emoto performed experiments with water throughout the 1990's. He had groups of people sit and stare at glasses of water. He asked some groups to think pleasant, happy thoughts; other groups he asked to think wicked, horrible, even murderous thoughts. Afterwards, he analyzed the water at a microscopic level. With the groups that were thinking loving, positive thoughts, the water crystals were brilliant and beautiful. They look like elegant, ornate snowflakes.

For the groups that were thinking murderous, hateful, and evil thoughts, the water crystals were malformed, yellow-rust in color, and ugly. The water in the various glasses was from the same source, the circumstances surrounding the experiment were the same for the different groups, only their thoughts were different. There were some instances where he examined polluted water and "clean" spring water. The results were similar to the thought experiments.

There was an experiment some years back called the double-slit experiment. This experiment demonstrated that light and matter can display characteristics of both waves and particles. How they were viewed was a function of how they were perceived. I'm not a scientist, nor do I play one on TV, so I'll tread lightly when talking about quantum mechanics. My understanding of the essence of quantum mechanics is that reality is how it's perceived. That sounds like a head-scratcher so let me go back to the double-slit experiment.

In essence, a wave passing through two narrow and parallel slits will form a pattern of interference on a screen; the wave is being disrupted. In light's case, light isn't just a wave, it's also a photon. When the scientists passed a single photon of light through the screen, it still displayed wave properties, appearing to go through both slits simultaneously. Things got weirder when the scientists realized their observation of the experiment changed the behavior of the photons.

If the observer in the experiment observed light behaving like a particle, that's because it was. If the observer saw it behaving like a wave, that's because it was. Huh?

We're not going to go from talking about Neo and the *Matrix* into a full-blown dissertation on the nature of quantum physics. I do want to extract the essence of my understanding of quantum mechanics into our discussion.

One elementary takeaway from the double-slit experiment is this – our thoughts shape our reality. This appears to be true when it comes to trying to determine if light is a wave or a particle, but let's take that smallest of examples and blow it up to life-size. Two people can look at the same thing and have a different experience while viewing it. Let's say two people are looking at a vase of red roses. One person looks at them and thinks of love. They think of their boyfriend or girlfriend, and the roses call to their mind a recent romantic moment the two shared. Their mood brightens. They smile and get excited about seeing their loved one soon.

The other person thinks of loss. For that person, the roses remind them of a family member who recently passed away. Their mood turns sour. They frown. Their face becomes downcast, and they feel the sorrow of their loved one's absence. Both of these individuals are having different experiences based on their perceptions of the world.

Thoughts then, are energy. That sounds crazy, doesn't it? It sounds crazy until you reflect on the examples we've discussed already. If you put your attention on something, you direct energy towards it, as evidenced by the water experiment. If you think about something that excites you, you create a certain kind of energy. Thinking about something that depresses you creates a different kind of energy.

If our thoughts shape our reality, but we're only actively "thinking" half the time, is it any wonder our lives seem vacant? If we spend a third of our lives physically asleep, and half of our waking lives mentally asleep, we're letting life happen to us. A life lived in this manner is a series of "almosts" and "could have beens." In light of this, it becomes easy to understand why we haven't been getting the results we want. In order to get the results we want, we have to think about what we want. We have to shift our perception from this idea that life happens to us and realize that life happens for us. If we want to live a more fulfilled life, we need to be present and active in our lives, and use our thoughts to shape our destiny. When we do this to realize our Purpose, that's our Purposeful Obsession.

Note here that I'm not saying to obsess on a thought. When you declare your Purpose to the universe, your mind scrambles around your Purpose like it's a Rubik's Cube. You'll start to think about different aspects of your Purpose. You'll begin to think of the steps needed to realize your Purpose. That's the beginning of your plan. That is Purposeful Obsession.

Henry Ford had it. Steve Jobs did as well. LeBron James seems to be obsessed with his legacy in the NBA and what he will leave behind in the City of Cleveland. Or Stan Lee, the creator of many of the most famous superheroes in comic book history. From the *Fantastic Four* to *Spiderman* to the *X-Men*, Stan Lee has left an indelible mark on pop culture. Was he purposefully obsessed with what he did at *Marvel Comics*? *Marvel Comics*, otherwise known as the "House of Ideas." What a great nickname for a company. I'd say Stan Lee is Purposefully Obsessed.

There are unhealthy obsessions... things we call addictions. Those have no place on our journey to realizing our Purpose.

SPINNING PLATES

The other big notion I want you to think about in our quantum journey on the power of thought is this ~ every man-made object ever produced was someone's thought. From this book in your hands, to your laptop computer, to a toothpick. Every single thing man has made was a thought before it came into existence. The power of our thoughts is one of the greatest gifts we have.

Knowing that our thoughts shape our reality, we need to take control of our minds. That seems a little silly, I know. Until you think about how much we daydream. And how much we defer decision making to someone else. How we just need time not to think, when what we really want is a break from all the noise we're being bombarded by. That noise is thought. Thoughts are generally passive, a conditioning. It's time to rein those thoughts back in. To turn off the mental cruise-control and take the wheel. What does this really mean?

To take another page from yoga, it means we need to be mindful. We need to be present. In yoga, to help us stay present, we focus on our breath. Away from the yoga mat, we aren't going to get more than twenty-four hours out of our day, so we need to make better choices in how we spend our time. That requires active thinking. That means doing something.

One analogy I like to use in my coaching practice is that of plates spinning on poles. We fill our lives with so many activities that put demands on our time and attention, it's like trying to keep dozens of plates spinning atop their poles. A plate over here starts to wobble, and we give our time and energy to it to keep it from crashing onto the ground. Then another plate over there gets a wobble, and we move to that plate to give it a spin. Then a third. We exhaust ourselves because we have too many spinning plates! Our takeaway from this is that all the spinning plates constitute a full life. And that's accurate. But a full life and a fulfilled life are not one and the same.

Everything can't be a priority. We can't be all things to all people. We need to let some plates wobble and fall. And that's okay. It's necessary. If we're to regain some time for realize our Purpose, we need to put some constraints on our lives. When we assess what's really important to us and what isn't in pursuit of our Purpose, we liberate our minds. This thinking calls to mind the old notion that it's better to do one thing exceptionally well than do a hundred things poorly.

Coming to grips with our Purpose and crafting the means by which it will be realized requires all of our mental faculties. We need healthier mental consumption habits. The good news is, realizing our life's Purpose helps foster those habits.

DESIRE AND ACTION

When you pause to think about it, our thoughts fall into two categories: desires or memories. We are either reflecting on something that happened, or thinking about something we want to have or to have happen. This can be debilitating if we let it.

Think about the last time you got into an argument with someone you were close to. What happened after the argument, particularly if things were left unresolved?

You kept thinking about it. You replayed it back in your mind, over and over again. You thought about what they said, or what you said. You thought about what you might have said differently, to help you get your point across more strongly, or to "win" the argument. Or worse, you feel guilty about what you said, and you're replaying the worst parts over in your head, reliving the "ouch" moments.

You worked yourself up into a kind of frenzy, and now your emotions are keeping your thoughts focused around that negativity. You're agitated, and uncomfortable, and yet you keep replaying the argument in your mind. It doesn't make sense. There is no benefit in rehashing the argument in our heads... you aren't going to change what was said, or the outcome. You're building a mental "bridge to nowhere" and yet you insist on doing it.

By being present, we can disconnect ourselves from replaying the fight. We can also "finish the story" in our heads, and win the fight. When we do this, we appreciate that nothing is really gained; our opponent may concede, but so what? What did we win? Nothing.

The thoughts we have around desire are where we want to spend our mental energy. Desire moves us to take action. When we desire something, we seek a realization of something imprinted in our psyche. When that desire is the fulfillment of our life's Purpose, that becomes the measuring stick against which thoughts, decisions, and habits are evaluated.

MIND MATTERS

Where we focus our mental energy matters. If we create thought patterns where we don't have enough – we don't have enough time, we don't have enough money, we don't have enough stuff, we wind up creating a thought habit of general dissatisfaction. It doesn't matter how good our job is, or if we're on vacation, or if we own two homes… it simply isn't enough.

Does this resonate with you? I remembered when I first left the Marines and joined Cisco. In the Marines, I hadn't spent that much time on email and most meetings we had were face to face. In Cisco, we lived by email. In Cisco, I might get in half a day the same number of emails it would have taken a week to get in the Marines. It was crazy.

Our meetings were virtual. My team was scattered across the country, and we might be lucky if we all came together twice a year. The pace was outrageous and I started thinking I didn't have enough time. There wasn't enough time during the workday, so I would turn my laptop on at night to get work done. Then, there wasn't enough time in the work-week. Sometimes I would travel and all the time spent flying and navigating airports ate in to my meeting time and getting things done. I started working weekends.

When it came time to take a vacation, I dreaded it. Instead of thinking about relaxing and unwinding, I was thinking about how quickly vacation was going to be over and I would be back, scrambling to catch up on emails and missed calls and meetings. And that's exactly how my vacation went. Whenever I got close to enjoying myself, I had a little alarm that went off in my head. "You've got three days left before you're back at it." Sometimes to try and quiet that voice, I would check email during vacation. So now, I was taking time off to do work. I had a lot of spinning plates.

Finally, I stepped back. I thought back to a lesson I learned while I was in the Marines. I was the Operations Officer for the Third Recruit Training

Battalion at the Marine Corps Recruit Depot in Parris Island, South Carolina. "The island that time forgot" as we used to call it.

The pace at the recruit depot is unforgiving. As an officer, I was there by 6 a.m. and usually left by 6 p.m. The drill instructors were there earlier and later, with one of them staying overnight with the recruits every night during the training cycle.

I got reprimanded once because I held my one hundred and twenty recruits five minutes longer than scheduled in a classroom to allow the instructor to make a point. I thought it was a great point he was making; the problem was, my recruits were scheduled to get haircuts right after class. The five minutes I made my recruits late meant that everyone else scheduled to get haircuts that day was also going to be late, which added five minutes no one could afford into that day's training schedule. Unforgiving.

The lesson was given to me by my boss, the battalion executive officer. I had been working regularly until 6:30 or 7 p.m for a few weeks, unable to dent the seemingly unending amount of work piled up on my desk. He came in one day on his way home and said, "go home. The work will be here for you when you get here tomorrow."

It made sense. No matter how much work I did in one day, no matter how late I stayed, there was always something waiting for me the next day. That lesson changed how I thought about work. How I thought about my time. It made for a much more satisfying work atmosphere, and a more fulfilled life. Even though Cisco was a different environment from the Marines, that lesson still applied.

After that, it became easier to unplug, and to be present during vacations. The only real thing that changed was how I thought about work.

ABUNDANCE

If we look at our life through a lens of inadequacy, then we're constantly setting ourselves up for disappointment. Instead, we need to focus our thoughts around what we have. We shouldn't look to compare what we have to what someone else has; we should be grateful for what we have.

EIGHT:
I HAVE GANESH ON SPEED-DIAL

"Acknowledging the good that you already have in your life
is the foundation for all abundance."

~ Eckhart Tolle

I can still remember the first time someone told me I had changed their life. We were meeting face to face for the first time after exchanging several emails concerning work. She represented a hiring firm and I was always on the lookout for reliable sources of finding new talent.

Our discussion started out along the usual lines of me explaining how my team was set up, and the kinds of qualities I looked for in new contractors or employees. She responded by telling me how her company had enjoyed considerable success in positioning people within my group, and how they could be flexible and responsive to any hiring needs we might have. In fact, they had previously found for us someone with hard-to-find skills where four other vendors with a three-month head start had failed.

The conversation was wrapping up, or so I thought, and we started talking about life away from work. She had been married a few years, and was raising a beautiful daughter who had recently celebrated her first birthday. When I mentioned teaching yoga, writing, coaching, and maintaining a full-time job, she asked me how I found the time for all these things while still being a dad and being in a relationship.

It opened up an amazing conversation about Purpose. I shared with her my thoughts on how we fill our lives with so much background noise, we mistake the noise for a meaningful life. And that inside each of us, we have this divine spark, this amazing gift we're meant to realize and to share with people.

Our time ran thirty minutes longer than scheduled, and as I walked her and her colleague out of the building, I told her I was grateful for her time, and that I looked forward to working with her team. She shook my hand and told me I had changed her life.

My initial thought was, people in our present day and age throw words around pretty casually. We say things like "that's hilarious" at something that is funny, but may not actually be full-on hilarious. Or we say, "George is the best person ever." George may be pretty great, but is he really the best person that's ever existed? I thought it was a nice way to close out our conversation, and the "thank you" I replied with indicated as much.

She was still holding my hand in the handshake, and put her other hand on top of it to get my attention. She squeezed my hand and said, "No. You've really changed my life." I was stunned. It was one of the most humbling experiences of my life, and I'm so grateful for that moment. The moment served as a bellwether for me in affirming my Purpose; to inspire people.

SEASONAL GRATITUDE

Gratitude is about being thankful and showing appreciation for people and events in our lives. Gratitude is about acknowledging connection, which underscores why it is a central theme in many of the world's religions.

In the Hindu religion, Ganesh is known as the remover of obstacles. For many of us, one of the main obstacles we face is the absence of gratitude from our lives.

Here in the United States, many of us associate gratitude with the holidays. Starting in November with Thanksgiving, we offer thanks for the family and friends who have meant so much to us over the previous year. We're a little nicer to one another. More thoughtful. We consciously open doors for people. Or when a door is opened for us, we acknowledge it by offering thanks. When the calendar turns to December, the feeling of gratitude grows, and we turn to the seasonal tradition of giving. It may be the giving of gifts, or it may be things more precious to us. We give our time by helping out at the local soup kitchen, or we donate our old clothes to Good Will. We do these things not because we're indebted to society, or to our families. We do them to show appreciation for others, even if some of those people are people we'll never see again or even meet. Then what happens after the holidays?

We toss out gratitude like it's something that also needs to be dropped off at *Goodwill.* January comes around. If family was in town, they've gone back home, or our kids are back at school or back to college. A month ago, we were looking forward to their visit; now we look back on it like it's something we had to endure. We survived another visit from the in-laws. We've rung in the New Year and the good feelings and sentiments we had over the holidays start to fade. We dread going back to work. Depending on where in the country we live, the weather might be crappy. The car looks dingy because of the mix of snow and the grime from the roads being treated. It's all just so... bleh! What happened? Why do we say goodbye to gratitude?

When we get to the core of what excites us about that time of year, is it the notion that we're going to get presents? That certainly has an appeal to us when we're younger, but as we get older, what we get at the holidays becomes less important.

Is it the realization that we're getting time off from work, or school? Those are welcome reliefs from routine, but hardly what actually gets us excited for the holidays. No. What excites us most about that time of year is it's time where we focus on giving. That is what we look forward to. It's this delicious gratitude cycle. We think about what we're going to give to others, or do for others without expecting anything in return. The fact that we get something in return, whether it's in the form of a gift or thoughtful sentiment, is icing on the gratitude cake!

Unfortunately for too many of us, we view this time of year and the feelings associated with it as just part of the schedule. We've told ourselves, in our busy, chaotic lives, "November and December... that's the time I've set aside to be 'extra' nice to people."

COMPLAINING IS MAINTAINING

Stop for a moment and think of all the things, all the people in your life. Think of your friends, your family members. Think of your coworkers. Now think of something about each of them to complain about. It's not hard to do, is it? This guy talks too much in trying to get to the point. She wears too much perfume in the office. He snores. She snores. We can think of tons of things to complain about.

If you have kids, how many times have you heard your child come in to the kitchen, open the pantry door or the refrigerator and say, "we don't have anything to eat"? What is your reaction? Are you kidding me? I just went to the grocery store! Never mind that the pantry and the refrigerator are both stocked with food.

We've gotten comfortable with complaining. For some of us, it's become our natural state. I would contend we've gotten comfortable with complaining BECAUSE we aren't living a life of Purpose.

We complain about what time we have to get up, about our lousy job. We complain about our stuff because our neighbor has better stuff. We complain about our spouse.

Why do we complain about our spouse? Well, we expect them to behave a certain way. We expect them to think the same way we do. We may have been attracted to them because of how different they were from us, or perhaps because of the similarities we shared. But boy, now that the shine has worn off, we find volumes of things to complain about.

Instead of appreciating them for who they are, we sabotage many of our relationships because of these expectations. Instead of being grateful for who our spouse is and the things they do, we complain about who they aren't and what they fail to do.

Complaining helps to reinforce the status quo. If we start to get outside our comfort zone, and insecurity and fear of change begin to rear their ugly heads, we "complain" ourselves back to where we want to be.

GRATITUDE AS DAILY RITUAL

Gratitude doesn't have to be something we resign ourselves to at a certain time of year; rather, it can be something we feel every day.

Think again about all the things and the people presently in your life. Now, instead of thinking of something to complain about, think of friends, family, and coworkers, and think about being grateful for them. She makes you smile with her funny stories. He's there whenever you need a hand.

Much like the vase of roses from the previous chapter, nothing has changed. They're still the same person they were when you were thinking of things to complain about. What's changed is your thinking towards them.

If complaining is the road with constant detours to our Purpose, gratitude is the smooth highway that will get us there with happiness to spare. Gratitude makes us feel better, because we're thinking good thoughts. It enhances the quality of our relationships; people want to be around a good-natured person. Does anyone like to hang out with the person who is complaining all the time? More than wanting to be around good-natured people, gratitude

If gratitude makes us appreciate the people in our lives, we begin to lose our expectations for people. Expectations in relationships are a road to disappointment. Marriages don't end because we appreciate someone for who they are. They end because we have this preconceived notion of what we should expect from our partner. After a while, they stop living up to that expectation.

Expectations are the bane of our existence. They become the framework by which we live our lives; they are the outline of our script. They are the road to angst and negativity.

When we express more gratitude in our lives, we have less room for negative emotions such as envy, hatred, and cynicism. When we marry a practice of gratitude with the Law of Attraction, we naturally bring more goodness into our lives.

Practicing gratitude makes us less self-absorbed. When we focus on the kindness of others, by definition we take our focus away from ourselves.

Gratitude needs to become a regular part of our routine. As much as I enjoy the practices of yoga and meditation, practicing gratitude has opened my eyes to the abundance of life. Like the other two practices, practicing gratitude helps me to be present, because it forces me to pay attention to what's happening around me.

Start the day off with gratitude. Identify three people or things you're grateful for every morning before you get out of bed. Bring gratitude into your dealings with others.

What do you usually think about before you go to bed? Are you worrying about your kids? Does your mind wander to the anxieties you think are waiting for you in the morning?

GRATITUDE AND PURPOSE

When it comes to realizing and manifesting our Purpose, we know that negative thoughts and negative energy will not benefit us. Those things will undercut our Purposeful Obsession and distract us.

On the flip side, positive thoughts and positive energy will, by definition, benefit us in the pursuit of our Purpose. Gratitude, then, is the key to a full life. Gratitude is the difference between saying, "this isn't enough" and "this is plenty." Between saying, "I refuse to accept this," and "I accept this for what it is".

Gratitude is not settling. It is not surrendering to the status quo. That was one of the misunderstandings I took away from yoga when I first started practicing it. We discussed how to quiet the mind and how to be fully present in order to gain enlightenment. My reaction to this was, "great, now what?" We just go around being enlightened all day? Just accepting life as it happens? That didn't sound very enlightened. It sounded like a recipe for being a passenger in life, and not a driver.

But what yoga is meant to do, coupled with a regular meditation practice, is to get you to a place where you can direct your mind and your energy towards accomplishing the things you want to accomplish. The premise behind clearing your mind is designed to wipe the slate clean and to provide clarity around what it is you're after.

If you look at the two negative sayings above, play those out to their conclusions. If you say, "this isn't enough," what follows that? For most people, what follows naturally is the thought or spoken words, "I want more." And what feeling does that evoke? Dissatisfaction. From being dissatisfied, we have a couple of choices. If we can get more, then we devise a plan to do that. If we can't get more, then we just get angry and frustrated. Both options are operating from a place of negativity. Even if we get more, we won't necessarily feel good about it.

If we say, "I refuse to accept this," that's a cold splash of denial. That immediately feels pretty negative. The strength of the denial suggests a foregone conclusion that we can't change the outcome. This leads down the not great rabbit hole of frustration and anger.

Now look at the two positive sayings. Both express contentment and satisfaction. Both express gratitude. If these sayings are being said in response to our pursuit of Purpose, they may not be the end state we're looking for, but they are positive road signs on the journey. "This is plenty," suggests happiness and gratitude for what we've received, while "I accept this for what it is," is recognizing a situation at face value. We might follow that by saying, "I can do better."

THE BASIC PERSONALITY TYPES

Several years ago, there was a popular cartoon strip called *The Far Side*, written and illustrated by Gary Larson. In one particularly memorable cartoon that my brother taped to our family refrigerator, there was a drawing of four people that was intended to represent the four personality types. My brother had scratched out the personality types and written instead "Mom" for the first person, "Dad" for the second, himself for the third, and me for the fourth. They were all looking at a glass of water. The first person was the optimist, saying the glass was half-full. The next one, the pessimist, said the glass was half-empty. The third was indecisive and couldn't make up his mind on whether or not the glass was half-full or half-empty. The fourth was the complainer. He looked at the glass and cried, "hey! I ordered a cheeseburger!"

I would offer a fifth personality type. The grateful personality. Someone who says, "hey look! I've got a glass of water."

PURPOSE AND DISRUPTION

Having a regular practice of gratitude becomes paramount when we come to grips with our Purpose. Realizing our Purpose will have a profound impact on our lives. Understanding our Purpose is like getting fitted with glasses to get our vision back to 20/20 after seeing life as a blurry series of events.

Pursuing our Purpose can be tremendously disruptive. As we align to our purpose and begin changing our thought processes, decisions, and habits, we start to change our lives. This has an impact on our relationships and work. This changes our focus. Our priorities. Communication with those close to us is paramount.

Imagine you decide your Purpose is you want to write screenplays. Maybe you dabbled in screenplay writing in college before you decided that was nothing more than a fanciful notion of your youth. Since then, you've gotten married, had three kids, and found a job you're comfortable in. How do you explain this?

Well, if you've shared a lot with your spouse, hopefully they know your love of screenplay writing. But what if you say you want to quit your job and throw yourself into screenplay writing? Your spouse might look at you like you've got a screw loose. If you quit your job, what does that do to your financial situation? Does your spouse work? Can their income cover all the bases while you undertake your life's Purpose? These things need to be discussed. The disruption can be very real.

NINE:

I HAVE SOMETHING IN MY THIRD EYE!

"Life is a series of experiences, each one of which makes us bigger,
even though sometimes it is hard to realize this.
For the world was built to develop character, and we must learn
that the setbacks and grieves which we endure
help us in our marching onward."

~ Henry Ford

My dad died unexpectedly in 2008, the Saturday before Thanksgiving. He had been the picture of health, going to the gym three times a week. He was relatively young when he passed away, only 68. We always look for meaning in death and, nine years later, I remain struck by the idea that he passed away at my parent's beach condo, sitting in a chair with a book, his bag packed on the bed ready for his trip. The idea still dances in my head, between logic and emotion. The logical part of my brain assesses those elements for what they were. He was reading a book before his drive back home when he died. The emotional side assesses those elements for what they *might* have been. He knew his time was coming and didn't want to "inconvenience" the family by dying in our presence. His bag was packed, ready for the journey where bags wouldn't be needed.

It was a sledgehammer to my life, and for my family. I missed weeks of work, and even when I returned, it took me months to really get back into a groove. When my 40th birthday arrived almost six months later, I felt old. Life was no longer fun. It was cruel and unforgiving.

113

I had a front row seat to the upheaval his passing had created for my mom. Thankfully, I lived only a few miles from my parents' house, and was able to provide some comfort for my mom while she grieved the loss of her husband, partner, and best friend. She misses him still, almost nine years after his death. So do I.

Much like bullets, tragedies don't discriminate. They happen to us all. The same is true for setbacks and the pitfalls of life. Eventually, we all experience the loss of people close to us. We may lose our job. Our home is damaged in a storm, or a fire. We might be committed in a relationship, only to find our partner isn't. Our child has a problem in school. These happenings are what a good friend of mine calls, the texture of life.

Our Purpose is not immune to such events when they happen. Our Purpose may or may not be divinely inspired, but it is only realized through our vision, our resolve, and our dedication. In an ideal world, we could invest whatever time and energy was needed to realize our Purpose without impacting those around us, or being affected by circumstances as they unfold in our lives. But no one's life operates in a vacuum. When life throws us a curveball, there can be very real consequences.

Our time and energy will be impacted. When my dad died, my focus shifted from getting ready for the holidays and spending time with family to notifying people of his passing and making funeral arrangements. I lost sleep. I lost weight. In the weeks that followed, my plans weren't focused weeks or months out. I was focused on getting through each day.

Setbacks are rarely scheduled. Because they aren't planned activities, when they happen it's like someone opened Pandora's box. We're slammed with a variety of questions, some of which don't have easy answers. Or worse, they don't have answers at all. What does this mean? How did this happen? Why did this happen?

The setback that we face may be directly related to our Purpose. It may be, we failed. How many times have we failed at something and given up? Through a lack of self-confidence and a lack of resolve, we have come to associate failure with things we tell ourselves aren't worth our time. As if to say, if this was something I was meant to do, I would have done it with the effort I put forward.

We have a negative attitude towards failure, which stems from connotations created through our education system. But failure is learning. When we fail in the pursuit of our Purpose, we're developing a better understanding of how to accomplish it.

With that in mind, we should expect setbacks. If we've stepped out of our comfort zone and are pursuing that thing that we've always wanted to do, we should welcome setbacks. We're operating outside our normal environment. Stretching ourselves. What makes us comfortable in our day to day lives are the routines we establish to try and minimize the chance that something unforeseen happens. But when we truly take control of our lives, every experience becomes more meaningful. This includes life's curveballs.

LET IT GO

There's a story I sometimes share at the beginning of a yoga class. The story is of two monks. They are walking on a path next to a river. At one point along their journey, they come across a beautiful, young woman. She is trying to get across the river, but the current is strong, and she is fearful. She asks if they can help her cross. The two monks look at one another, as they had both taken a vow never to touch a woman.

The older monk steps forward, puts the woman on his back, and carries her across the river. His companion looks at him with disdain. He cannot believe what the older monk is doing. The younger monk crosses the river, and the two part ways with the woman. They continue their walk.

An hour passes. Then two more. Finally, after four hours, the young monk cannot stay quiet any longer.

"We are not allowed to be with a woman. How, then, could you put that woman on your back and carry her across the river?"

The older monk says, "brother, I left the woman back at the river crossing. Why are you carrying her still?"

No one wants bad things to happen to them in life. We don't go consciously looking for misfortune to smack us around a bit. But when it happens, we wrestle with it. We dwell on it, causing ourselves more heartache and discomfort. *No! Why did this have to happen?* We spend energy wishing with all our might it hadn't happened.

Moments in life hurt when we can't accept things as they are. We don't want a relationship to end. We don't want to say goodbye. We hold on to our grief, trying to undo things that can't be undone. Our inability to let go prevents us from moving forward.

Because we don't plan for these things to happen, we don't have a good idea on how to deal with them when they do. Dealing with them means setting a timetable around which we'll let them occupy our time, focus, and energy. When that time comes to an end, agree to accept the new reality. This doesn't mean our emotions automatically go away, but it's an agreement with ourselves to redirect our focus back to Purpose.

EMOTIONS AND INTELLECT

We make decisions from one of two sources: our intellect and our emotions. Not all setbacks will trigger an emotional response or, more accurately, not all setbacks should trigger an emotional response. When something doesn't work, emotions won't tell us why. If we listen too much to our emotions, self-doubt will begin to creep in. A setback can be a body blow to our ego and to our confidence. The emotional part of ourselves, if we listen to it, will turn each jab at our confidence into a haymaker.

Intellect will tell us why something didn't work. If it's a lesson towards our Purpose, understanding why something didn't work is important. When we take the emotion out of a situation, we can be objective. The facts become clear, and we can take steps to prevent ourselves from making the same mistakes in the future.

Earlier, I mentioned the definition of insanity as doing the same thing but expecting different results. This will undoubtedly happen in pursuit of our Purpose. Something won't work, or we won't get the results we expect. Don't try harder. Change our approach. Over and over. And over. Until we see the results we want.

STAY ON PURPOSE

One of my fonder memories from college was riding my motorcycle. I enjoyed my motorcycle immensely, even though I'd never taken a safety course, and didn't really understand how to ride correctly. Because I didn't understand how to ride, I spilled my bike on several occasions, earning the nickname "Crash" from my friends. To top off the level of my ignorance, I had a Kawasaki Ninja. If you don't know a lot about bikes, let's just say that the Ninja isn't a great bike for cross-country travel.

At the end of my junior year of college, it was time for me to head home to start preparing for Officer Candidates School. The Penn State Spring Semester ended pretty earlier compared to other schools, and the first weekend of May, I started the long trip south. My parents were living in Southern Georgia at the Marine Corps Logistics Base in Albany, and it would take me a solid two days of full riding to make it home.

I wound my way through Pennsylvania and made it in to Virginia. In the early part of the afternoon, I hit a rainstorm. Rain and motorcycles don't mix too well, so I elected to stop for the day. I found a cheap motel, grabbed a late lunch and settled in to watch the NBA playoffs. I reasoned that I would get before dawn the next morning and knock the rest of the trip out.

When I woke the next morning, the temperature was thirty-one degrees. A cold front had blown in. I had my helmet, jeans, a t-shirt, and a jean jacket. Not ideal for traveling in freezing temperatures. The problem was, I'd already checked out of the motel. And I was determined to get home.

I started riding and my hands got numb within minutes. I found a truck stop and stopped to go inside. After ten minutes, I tried again. The same thing happened. My hands were getting numb. I found a 7-11 and bought trucker's gloves and a paper-thin Washington Redskins sweatshirt. My legs were getting cold quickly too, so I reasoned I had to do something about them.

I went into the bathroom, dropped my jeans and triple-wrapped toilet paper around my legs, then pulled my jeans back up. I got back on the bike and started riding. It was still freezing and the sun wasn't up yet, but I was able to ride for nearly half an hour before the cold became too much to bear.

I found another rest stop and decided to try and sleep until the sun rose, so at least there would be a little more warmth. After about ninety minutes of fitful sleep, the sun was up and so was I.

I was able to ride now, even though it was still really cold. I rode for at least an hour, making my way through part of the Blue Ridge Mountains. Then I hit snow. I kept on.

Finally, after what seemed like an eternity, I made it out of the snow and in to North Carolina. It was early afternoon now, and things were warmer. At one of my many stops, I'd heard that, in addition to the chilly temperatures, there were gale force wind warnings the further south you went. I found that to be true in North Carolina, but made it through the state without much trouble.

One of the stark differences between North and South Carolina is the number of trees along the highway. Going down Interstate 85 in North Carolina, the tree line is just off the highway. This served to lessen the strength of the wind gusts. In South Carolina, there weren't many trees along the highway.

I found myself leaning into the wind to drive straight. Just after four that afternoon, I stopped at a rest stop to rest. It was nice enough out that I found a nice grassy hill and allowed myself twenty minutes of down-time before I hopped back on the bike.

I went for another hour when trouble smacked me right in the face. Trouble in the form of the wind shear coming off the front of an eighteen-wheeler. I moved into the passing lane to pass a semi ahead of me. As I came up on his cab, the strength of the wind coming off the front of his truck was strong enough to "push" me into the median.

I remember looking down as the bike went off the road and passed over the gravel. I was thinking, braking here seems like a bad idea. The bike continued onto the grass by the guardrail. I was able to straighten it out so I wasn't going to hit the guardrail, but I couldn't avoid the large rock in front of me. The bike hit the rock and I flew over the handlebars.

I did a complete head-over-heels flip and landed on my back. There were stars in my eyes, but once they cleared, I did a quick check. I had a bruise on my left hand, otherwise I was unscathed. The bike was less fortunate.

The forks holding the front wheel had been jarred out of alignment, and the foot-brake had twisted underneath itself. My ride was over. The trucker kept on going.

I made my way to a diner half a mile down the road and phoned home. I explained the situation to my dad, who would have to borrow someone's pickup to retrieve the bike. There was still six hours between us. He made it to me by midnight and, after retrieving the bike from the local wrecker, we made it home just after six the following morning. It was ugly, but I made it home.

Setbacks are a part of life. Don't allow yourself to get frustrated when they happen. Your life's Purpose is your greatest "why..." the "how" of it may vary from time to time.

TEN:

EMBRACE THE POSSIBLE

"Sutra 32: The practice of concentration on a single object is the best way to prevent obstacles and their accompaniments."

– Sri Patanjali, The Yoga Sutras of Patanjali

Banyan trees are native to India and are part of the ficus family. They have deep roots, and some trees are known to be over two hundred years old. If you're unfamiliar with the banyan tree, as the tree grows, aerial roots drop down from its branches. These roots run deep into the soil and over time become large enough to be mistaken for tree trunks themselves. Come across a large enough tree, and the effect is like walking through a forest of banyan trees.

Banyan trees are impressive in that, wherever the roots hang down and burrow into the earth, their connection is solid. It isn't a delicate tree. And nothing in nature seems indecisive. The banyan is a tree with purpose.

In the continental United States, the largest banyan tree is located in Ft. Myers, Florida. The tree was planted in 1925 and, at the time of its planting, was just four feet tall. Today, 92 years after it was planted, the tree stands over sixty feet tall and has a girth that exceeds thirty feet. The tree was planted by Thomas Edison and can be seen at his vacation home. His neighbor in Ft. Myers was none other than Henry Ford.

We owe so much to Thomas Edison and Henry Ford. While Edison favored painstakingly exhaustive trial and error, Ford preferred Edison brought us the stock printer and the alkaline battery. He invented the phonograph. When asked about failing 1,000 times in producing the light bulb, he famously said, "I didn't fail 1,000 times. The light bulb was an invention with 1,000 steps".

Growing up, Henry Ford idolized Thomas Edison. Ford didn't create the first V-8 engine, but he created a relatively inexpensive one. He did this with a team of engineers who, upon hearing his initial ask and constraints, told him it was impossible. Ford would check in with these engineers from time to time, hearing them reiterate time and again the impossibility of his ask. He would thank them for the feedback, and ask them to let him know when they'd created what he'd asked. Finally, Ford persevered, and the impossible became possible. This was a man who said, "whether you think you can, or whether you think you can't, you're right."

What can YOU do? What are you capable of? The life you've always wanted is right in front of you. See it. Feel it. Clear out the junk mail of your life. Run out of excuses.

Think. Really think. Thomas Edison once said, "five percent of the people think, ten percent of the people think they think, and the other eighty-five percent would rather die than think." Be part of that five percent.

Believe in your Purpose. Believe in yourself. Believe that the life you've always imagined, the life that exists within your mind can exist in reality. In order to change your life, to realize your Purpose, you have to believe you can change. Make decisions that build towards realizing that Purpose. You will be astonished at how much clarity you gain when you put your Purpose at the forefront of your thoughts. It needs to stay there, it needs to be tended to. Make it start with one simple habit. Wake up thirty minutes earlier. Then, add in meditation. A meditation that breaks down the walls you've boxed your life into. Rewrite your script. Realize that, in this universe of vibrating atoms, anything you set your mind to is possible. There are masterminds that have taken the path you want to follow. Find them. Learn from them.

Your Purpose is your gift to the world. Now is the time to share it.

ACKNOWLEDGEMENTS

In any creative endeavor, we are never truly alone, and that there are those who, directly or indirectly, lend a helping hand. That is certainly true in the bringing to life this book.

Thanks to Margaret Dowis for leading me down the path of becoming a yoga instructor, to Jean Gennaro for challenging me to up my game as a writer. Thanks also to Tyson Swanger for convincing me to get back on a bike. Josh Edwards, for helping me see the difference between an amateur writer and a professional one. Mark Calaway, for helping me understand how to embrace the "texture" of life. Bob Proctor, though we have yet to meet, for pointing me in the direction of James Allen and Napoleon Hill. Peggy McColl, your insights, mentoring and counsel have been invaluable. I'm eternally grateful for all the paths you've illuminated.

Tremendous thanks to Judy O'Beirn, Jenn Gibson, and the amazingly talented people at Hasmark Publishing.

Finally, deep, heartfelt thanks to Jenna Mattran. Your love, patience, and understanding are realized in these pages. Thank you, a thousand times over. I have more poems to write.

NOTES

ONE: GET ME OUTTA THIS CASK!

Whiskey History:
https://www.scotchwhiskyexperience.co.uk/about-whisky/history

Top 7 Surprising Benefits of Whiskey:
https://www.organicfacts.net/health-benefits/beverage/whiskey.html

The Benefits of Yoga:
http://www.osteopathic.org/osteopathic-health/about-your-health/
health-conditions-library/general-health/Pages/yoga.aspx

TWO: THE HAPPINESS BUZZ

What is Happiness, Anyway?:
Parks, Acacia https://my.happify.com/hd/what-is-happiness-anyway/

Philosophy of Happiness:
https://en.wikipedia.org/wiki/Philosophy_of_happiness

The 4 "Happy Hormones":
http://www.joyfuldays.com/happy-hormones/

Bureau of Labor Statistics:
https://www.bls.gov/spotlight/2016/self-employment-in-the-united-states/
pdf/self-employment-in-the-united-states.pdf

Oxford, Cliff. "Where the Happy Talk About Corporate Culture is Wrong." *The New York Times* 7 May 2013 Web. 7 May 2013

Why work? A psychologist explains the deeper meaning of your daily grind: Quito, Ann. https://qz.com/498951/why-work-a-psychologist-explains-the-deeper-meaning-of-your-daily-grind/

Why Do We Work?: Hudson, Paul http://elitedaily.com/money/entrepreneurship/why-do-we-work/

U.S. Employee Engagement: http://www.gallup.com/poll/180404/gallup-daily-employee-engagement.aspx

Entertainment Software Association (2016) *Essential Facts About the Computer and Video Game Industry* [PDF file]. Retrieved from: http://essentialfacts.theesa.com/Essential-Facts-2016.pdf

Weinschenk, Susan (2012, Sept 11) *Why We're All Addicted to Texts, Twitter and Google*. Retrieved from: https://www.psychologytoday.com/blog/brain-wise/201209/why-were-all-addicted-texts-twitter-and-google

McDonald, Emma (2017, Apr 20) *The Global Games Market Will Reach $108.9 Billion in 2017 With Mobile Taking 42%*. Retrieved from: https://newzoo.com/insights/articles/the-global-games-market-will-reach-108-9-billion-in-2017-with-mobile-taking-42/

Marvel Cinematic Universe at the Box Office. Retrieved from: http://www.boxofficemojo.com/franchises/chart/?id=avengers.htm

United Problem Solvers (2016) *UPS Pulse of the Online Shopper White Paper*. Retrieved from: https://solvers.ups.com/ups-pulse-of-the-online-shopper/

Scrape Hero (2017, Jan 4) *How Many Products are Sold on Amazon.com – January 2017 Report*. Retrieved from: https://www.scrapehero.com/how-many-products-are-sold-on-amazon-com-january-2017-report/

McLellan, Laura and Sorofman, Jake (2015, Feb. 13) *CMO Spend Survey 2015: Eye on the Buyer*. Retrieved from: https://www.gartner.com/doc/2984821/cmo-spend-survey--eye

Henry Wechsler, Ph.D., and Toben F. Nelson, Sc.D. What We Have Learned from the Harvard School of Public Health College Alcohol Study: *Focusing Attention on College Student Alcohol Consumption and the Environmental Conditions That Promote It.* Department of Society, Human Development and Health, Harvard School of Public Health, 677 Huntington Avenue, Boston, Massachusetts 02115

THREE: CONSUMPTION OVERLOAD TO GO, PLEASE

Marine Corps University Foundation School of Advanced Warfighting. Retrieved from:
http://www.mcuf.org/mcu_saw.html

Wallace, Kelly (2015, Nov. 3) *Teens spend a 'mind-boggling' nine hours a day using media, a report says.* Retrieved from:
http://www.cnn.com/2015/11/03/health/teens-tweens-media-screen-use-report/index.html

U.S. Food and Drug Administration (2013) Guidance for Industry: A Food Labeling Guide (14. Appendix F: Calculate the Percent Daily Value for the Appropriate Nutrients) Retrieved from:
https://www.fda.gov/Food/GuidanceRegulation/GuidanceDocuments-RegulatoryInformation/LabelingNutrition/ucm064928.htm

SIX: OM-M-G, YOU NEED A PLAN

Satchidananda, Swami (2012). *The Yogi Sutras of Patanjali/Translation and Commentary by Swami Satchidananda* Buckingham, VA: Integral Yoga Publications

SEVEN: DHYANA CHECK OUT MY ASANA?

The title is a semi-nonsensical play on words, using two Sanskrit words. "Dhyana" is seen as deep, profound meditation that is the quintessential degree of yoga, while "Asana" refers to a seated posture in which the person is sitting firm, but relaxed.

DR. EMOTO'S WATER EXPERIMENTS. The internet is replete with both videos and written overviews of Dr. Emoto's water experiments. A comprehensive overview of his studies and their results can be found at: http://www.masaru-emoto.net/english/water-crystal.html

DOUBLE-SLIT EXPERIMENT – there's a danger when a Liberal Arts major attempts to understand and communicate something as wildly baffling as quantum physics. While much of what I wrote regarding the subject was from memory, I did some verification at: Thompson, Avery (2016 Aug. 11) *The Logic-Defying Double-Slit Experiment is Even Weirder Than You Thought*. Retrieved from:

http://www.popularmechanics.com/science/a22280/double-slit-experiment-even-weirder/

EIGHT: I HAVE GANESH ON SPEED-DIAL

The Four Personality Types. I don't have anything compelling to say about this, other than it's worth looking up. *The Far Side* is timeless.

TEN: EMBRACE THE POSSIBLE

Edison and Ford Winter Estates *Edison and Ford Winter Estates*. Retrieved from:

http://www.edisonfordwinterestates.org/collections/biographies/edison-ford-winter-estates/

ABOUT THE AUTHOR

 A Harley enthusiast, firewalker, yoga teacher, life coach, and drinker of fine scotches, David Richards is currently a senior manager with Technical Support at Cisco Systems. He was formerly a delivery manager to Cisco's Navy and Marine Corps accounts and the service delivery executive to the Department of Veterans Affairs. He served as an Officer of Marines, rising to the rank of Major and participated in both Operation RESTORE HOPE and Operation DESERT STORM. He received his Bachelors of English from Penn State University, and received two Masters degrees from Marine Corps University, with a PhD in Life. He lives in North Carolina.

The Literary Fairies

we make your literary wish come true

David Richards

has partnered with

The Literary Fairies

who have a mission to give to those who have
experienced an adversity or disability an opportunity
to become a published author while sharing
a story to uplift, inspire and entertain the world.

Visit TLF website to find out how YOU
could become a published author or where
you can help grant a literary wish.

More details provided at
www.theliteraryfairies.com

Made in the USA
Middletown, DE
03 October 2017